"PULLED OFF AT HALF-TIME"

Sir Alf Ramsey:

"I'll be watching you for the first 45 minutes
and if you don't work harder
I'll pull you off at half-time."

Rodney Marsh:

"Christ! At Man City we only get a cup of tea
and an orange!"

" PULLED OFF AT HALF-TIME "

by Stuart Reeves

with a foreword by Rodney Marsh

CARLTON

This edition published in 2007 by
Carlton Books Limited,
20 Mortimer Street, London W1T 3JW

10 9 8 7 6 5 4 3 2 1

A CIP catalogue record for this book is
available from the British Library.

ISBN: 978-1-84442-257-9

Project Art Editor: Luke Griffin
Designer: Craig Stevens
Picture Research: Paul Langan
Production: Peter Hinton
Editorial: Jo Murray

Printed in United Kingdom

CONTENTS

FOREWORD

Let's face it, we all love it when one of our heroes
(or even someone we don't particularly like) makes
a faux pas.

Whether it's during a television, newspaper or radio
interview, at an after-dinner speech or just a retold story
by a so-called "friend", we can't help but chuckle
when a football personality screws up or gives us a
memorable quote.

I've had my share over the years and probably have
one or two still left in my locker. Many people say I gave
the "world champion" of one-liners from which this book
is entitled. I know most of the people who are quoted in
this brilliant book and I can bet not one is ashamed of
being included.

So enjoy the read and remember, we all make mistakes.
That's why they put rubbers on the end of pencils.

Rodney Marsh

INTRODUCTION

The great Tottenham Hotspur manager Bill Nicholson
once had this to say on the subject of intelligence
in footballers:

"Intelligence doesn't make you a good footballer.
Oxford and Cambridge would have the best sides if
that were true. It's a football brain that matters and
that doesn't usually go with an academic brain. I prefer
players not to be too good or too clever at other things.
It means they concentrate on football."

Now there are certainly plenty of examples to
back this up but it could also be applied to managers,
commentators and pundits alike. Often though, football
people come up with the smartest quips, wisecracks
and one-liners that any academic or poet laureate would
be proud of, and that – along with the usual mixed-
metaphors, general confusion, mangling of language
and post-match interview cliches – is what this book is
all about!

Stuart Reeves

GIFT OF THE GAB

"Apparently when you head a football, you lose brain cells, but it doesn't bother me... I'm a horse. No one's proved it yet have they?"
David May

"I would not sign for another club, not even for 15 million dollars. However, it would be different if they were to instead offer me 15 different women from all around the world. I would tell the club chairman: 'Please let me make these women happy – I will satisfy them like they have never been satisfied before.'"
Sasa Curcic lays down his terms for a move away from Aston Villa

"The neighbours on one side have got a villa in Portugal, the other side have got a house in America. We're looking for one in Filey (Yorkshire)." **David Batty**

"My dad does know Romeo from the group and he's played in a few bands with him. But my dad was definitely not the drummer in Showaddywaddy."
Dion Dublin debunks a great football myth

"Well, I rose like a salmon at the far post, but
Pally rose like a fresher salmon and towered
above me, headed the ball at the keeper,
the keeper fumbled, then I saw a sudden flash
of brilliant red and leathered it into the roof
of the net with my left foot sponsored by
Diadora boots."

**David May's vivid description of his goal in
Manchester United's 4–0 win over Porto in
March 1997**

"I'll get in trouble with my girlfriend if I play –
I don't think she'll be too happy if I'm chasing
Totti all over Rome."

**Jonathan Woodgate on his chances of making
only his second start for Leeds United, away
to AS Roma in the UEFA Cup in 1998**

"The White Pelé? You're more like the
White Nellie!"

**Bill Shankly as Peter Thompson struggled
to reproduce his international form in Brazil
on the domestic stage**

"I am quite a gruesome person. I did have a scrapbook on the Yorkshire Ripper… That was one of my most treasured possessions."
David Batty

"I'm very passionate about antiques because they are like people. You can learn a lot from them."
Emmanuel Petit

Police officer: "Mr McCoist, do you have a police record?"
Ian Durrant: "'Walking on the Moon'…"
From Ian Durrant's autobiography

Interviewer: "What do you say to the rumour that Gary Neville has been stealing bodies from graveyards and building some kind of creature from the parts in his garage?"
Denis Irwin: "I don't think it's Nev. He just lays up in his house all day. If you'd said any other player then maybe…"
A spoof interviewer from the *Mick Molloy Show* livens up a Manchester United press call in Australia in summer 1999

"I'll tell you what my real dream is. I mean my absolute number one dream that will mean I die a happy man if it happens. I want to see a UFO. They're real. I don't care if you look at me like that. UFOs are a definite fact and I've got to see one soon."

Paul Gascoigne bewilders some journalists

"If, as some people think, there is such a thing as reincarnation, I'd love to come back as an eagle. I love the way eagles move, the way they soar, the way they gaze."

Eric Cantona

"In English, the things you use in casinos
are chips, but in Italian we call them fish.
So I once said, 'When the fish are down...'
Everybody was, like, 'What are you
talking about?'"
**Gianluca Vialli on his attempts to conquer
the local lingo**

"Luca [Vialli] thinks he looks like Bruce Willis,
but I think he looks more like Bruce Forsyth."
Aaron Lincoln, Chelsea kitman in 1999

"Every time I see him it reminds me to buy a
pint of milk on the way home."
**More from Aaron Lincoln, this time on striker
Mikael Forssell's pale features**

"A survey was conducted of the world's
female population asking them if they would
sleep with Bill Clinton. 80 per cent of them
answered, 'What, again?'"
Peter Schmeichel tells a joke

"John Bond has blackened my name with his insinuations about the private lives of football managers. Both my wives are upset."
Malcolm Allison

"On the pitch, when I see green or smell green, I get a little bit crazy. The grass, you know? I get this green mist."
Jimmy Floyd Hasselbaink

"After you've scored a goal it's just orgasmic … if you asked me just after a game I'd says its better than sex, but if you asked me just after sex I'd say, 'Forget it, mate.'"
Trevor Sinclair on scoring – one way or the other

"The thing about sport, any sport, is that swearing is very much part of it."
Jimmy Greaves

"You've got to take the rough with the smooth. It's like love and hate, war and peace, all that boll*cks."
A bit of philosophy from Ian Wright

"Dogs are very honest. They'll never let you down. They'll play football with you in the garden … and at the end they'll crap all over your lawn."
Mark Viduka

"I've seen myself referred to as 'a legend'. I've been called worse, let's put it that way."
Robbie Fowler

"I'd certainly like to be as, er, big as Lara Croft one day."
Michael Owen at the launch of his own computer game

"I would like to be in a movie. I want to be the bad person who is killed at the end of the movie, like Gary Oldman in *Air Force One*."
Frank Leboeuf

"It won't be long before he has our supporters hanging from the rafters."
Alan Ball predicting a bright future for new signing Gio Kinkladze in 1995

"My mother wanted me to be a folk dancer, so when my father went to Russia to work for three years she hid away my football boots and took me to dancing classes."
Gio Kinkladze

"Sorry, Mr Chairman, but this is the earliest I have been late for some time."
Ally McCoist apologizes to Rangers chairman David Murray

"No comment, lads – and that's off the record."
Ally McCoist to a group of reporters during a Rangers media ban

"I'm often asked how this Rangers team compares with the Lisbon Lions. I have to be honest and say I think it would be a draw but, then, some of us are getting on for 60."
Glasgow Celtic great, Bertie Auld in 1993, after city rivals Rangers had reached the group stage of the Champions League for the first time

"We like Scotland because we love shortbread. Coming here is interesting to him."
Nivaldo Baldo, adviser to Brazilian Celtic trialist Marcio Amoroso back in 2004

"We signed to play until the day we died, and we did."
Jimmy Greaves speaks on radio, not from beyond the grave

"Two things struck me straight away. The standard of José's English and the fact that he was a nice-looking boy. Too good-looking for my liking."
Sir Bobby Robson, 2005

"I speak a bit of English so in the dressing room I knew that Mourinho's translations weren't literal. It was Robson, plus Mourinho's own observations. And they made sense."
Former Barcelona player Oscar Garcia reveals how José Mourinho dealt with the difficult job of translating for Sir Bobby Robson

"The moral of the story is not to listen to those who tell you not to play the violin but to play the tambourine."
José Mourinho has a Cantona moment, 2005

"I've never been a goalscorer, only own goals. Good own goals."
Arsenal's Steve Bould

"As far as I'm concerned, Tony [Adams] is like the Empire State Building."
Ian Wright

"To play for the club you support is a dream come true."
Ashley Cole on Arsenal before the dream turned sour

"Bottle is a quality too, you know. It's not just about ball control and being clever. Sometimes you have to show the world what's between your legs."

Graeme Souness

"As the ball came over, I remembered what Graham Taylor said about my having no right foot, so I headed it in."

John Barnes scoring against Taylor's Aston Villa in a 1988 FA Cup tie

"The best Italian this club has signed is the chef."

Frank Leboeuf on Chelsea

"Nobody hands you cups on a plate."

Terry McDermott, assistant to Kevin Keegan at Newcastle United

"She [Eileen Drewery] gives the players a shoulder to talk to."

Neil Webb

"I can see the carrot at the end of the tunnel."

Stuart Pearce

"Short back and sides."
Unidentified England player to Glenn Hoddle's faith healer Eileen Drewery

"Once you've had a bull terrier, you never want another dog. I've got six bull terriers, a Rottweiler and a bulldog."
Julian Dicks

"He'd no alternative but to make a needless tackle."
Chelsea and Celtic defender Paul Elliott

"I was disappointed to leave Spurs, but quite pleased that I did."
Steve Perryman

"I spent four indifferent years at Goodison, but they were great years."
Martin Hodge

"I always used to put my right boot on first, and then obviously my right sock."
Barry Venison

"I can't even remember when the Seventies was."
Robbie Keane

"You don't need balls to play in a cup final."
Steve Claridge

"I was born in Newcastle and I've played for Newcastle Schoolboys all my life."
The forever-young Dennis Tueart

"Paul Scholes – the most complete mental player I've ever seen."
Former Manchester United trainee Ben Thornley

"I'm as happy as I can be – but I have been happier."
Aston Villa and Middlesbrough defender Ugo Ehiogu

"I find the growing intervention by the football authorities in strictly footballing matters a rather worrying trend."
Kenny Cunningham wishes the FA would stay out of football

"You can't do better than a goal on your first start."

Bobby Zamora

"I took a whack on my left ankle, but something told me it was my right."

Lee Hendrie

"Left alone with our own heads on, we can be pretty mental."

Tony Adams

"I was surprised, but I always say nothing surprises me in football."

Les Ferdinand

"I was watching the Blackburn game on TV on Sunday when it flashed on the screen that George [Ndah] had scored in the first minute at Birmingham. My first reaction was to ring him up. Then I remembered he was out there playing."
Ade Akinbiyi

"It's a no-win game for us. Although I suppose we can win by winning."
Gary Doherty

"He'll be the leader in the tool kit."
Robbie Earle doesn't say which tool it is

"We could be putting the hammer in Luton's coffin."
Ray Wilkins

"The Championship is the carrot at the end of the Championship."
Tony Cottee

"It was a game of two halves, literally."
Chris Powell

"I faxed a transfer request to the club at the beginning of the week, but let me state that I don't want to leave Leicester."
Stan Collymore

"I was both surprised and delighted to take the armband for both legs."
Gary O'Neil

"I've always been a childhood Liverpool fan, even when I was a kid."
Harry Kewell

"He's started anticipating what's going to happen before it's even happened."
Graeme Le Saux

"In the last ten minutes I was breathing out of my ar*e."
Clinton Morrison

"Now the world is my lobster."
Keith O'Neill

TRAINING

"In training Jack would sometimes set the dogs on us!"

Stan Cummins recalls one of Jack Charlton's more bizarre training rituals at Middlesbrough

"Carlton Palmer can trap the ball further than I can kick it."

Ron Atkinson works on his player's close control

"I don't think I could jump over a car now – at my age, I'm grateful to be able to jump in one."

Everton's Duncan McKenzie, who developed the habit of jumping over Minis on the training ground

"Because of his pride, Hoddle wanted to be the best player in training every day – at 46 years of age. I don't think you can see the whole picture when you're training out there among the guys. Can you imagine Arsène Wenger playing with Thierry Henry and the rest?"

David Pleat

"I am a scientist. My training is brilliant and, like all scientists, I can make things work."
Malcolm Allison

"In training it was the English versus the Scots. Coisty came in our team because, as I told him at the time, he had played two games for the Sunderland reserves."
Terry Butcher on life at Rangers

"They had professors running the course. One of them told me that he wanted me to shoot at goal from a distance. The Portsmouth goalkeeper was in goal and I beat him and scored. The professor then came up to me and told me that I hadn't kicked the ball right."
Micky Fenton, scorer of 162 goals for Middlesbrough, on the boffins at a Birmingham University coaching course

"A Ferrari without a garage."
Italian journalist Giovanni Galavotti describes Fabrizio Ravanelli training at Middlesbrough's less than glamorous facilities

"We used to play with smoke from the
chimneys polluting the pitch. The pollution was
so bad I didn't even send my son to school."
Fabrizio Ravanelli

"I played my way into the side when I had a
good training session the day before the derby
match. I kicked a few of the lads and the
manager saw that."
**Middlesbrough's Lee Cattermole, then
17, explains how he earned his debut
at Newcastle**

"Some people might think we are lazy, but that's fine. What's the point of tearing players to pieces in the first few days? We never bothered with sand dunes and hills and roads; we trained on grass, where football is played."
Bill Shankly on pre-season training

"If I told people that the secret of Liverpool's success is a dip in the Mersey three times a week, I not only reckon they'd believe me but I think our river would be full of footballers from all over the country."
Liverpool trainer Ronnie Moran

"I hate training, I hate running, but at Liverpool they say if you don't put it in at training, how do you expect to put it in during a match?"
Robbie Fowler

"They are all like prostitutes: they smoke, they're lazy and they sleep all day."
Franz Beckenbauer on the Bayern Munich squad

"Respect for the club, for its norms, for its philosophy etc., is much more important than any other individual. The document I drew up, and which some now refer to as the 'Bible', is totally in line with this principle."
José Mourinho, talking about his famous biblical training manual

"Music from the Victor Sylvester Dance Orchestra echoed across the pitch from the Tannoy and we were ordered by the major to take our partners… The dancing was supposed to improve our rhythm and make us play like Brazilians. It didn't, we just fell about and he scrapped the idea in favour of hypnotism."
John Charles recalls the unorthodox training methods employed at Leeds United by "Major" Frank Buckley

"That's the way I am and I always will be. After all, I kick Laurent Robert in training – and he's one of our players."
Newcastle United's Andrew Griffin on his no-nonsense philosophy

"Seriously, I was the only player at Ajax who used to have fried eggs for breakfast every day. It's one of my superstitions. If I don't have a fried breakfast in the morning, I won't play or train well."

The secret of Marc Overmars' success

"Training was terribly slack. Players strolled up at any old time. Some would just walk round the track and one used to go over the far side for a smoke."

Peter McParland, scorer in the 1957 FA Cup final, describes life at Aston Villa in the 1950s

VICTORY

"Kenny Dalglish came on at the same time as me and everyone expected him to win it for Liverpool. But here I was, a ginger-haired nobody, setting up the winning goal for Arsenal."
Perry Groves on the 1987 League Cup final win over Liverpool

"It got to the point where I just thought, 'I'm going to take everyone on.' And when I got through I just hit it as hard as I could. David Seaman got a lot of stick, but it really was the only place I could have put it to beat him."
Ryan Giggs describing his wonder goal in the 1999 FA Cup semi-final replay against Arsenal

"Ryan just put his head down, ran like he always does, didn't pass and got lucky."
Nicky Butt's view of Giggs' goal

"It's great to get the first trophy under the bag."
Michael Owen

"The familiar sight of Liverpool lifting the League Cup for the first time…"
Barry Davies

"That will always be a memory for everyone
else I suppose. The winner's medal and
scoring the goal are my memories."
**Steve Morrow reflects on being dropped by
Tony Adams and breaking his collar bone after
the 1993 League Cup final replay**

"Before we won the Championship, I told the
lads exactly how many goals we would score
and how many points. I was exactly right.
I'm brilliant!"
**Manchester City manager Malcolm Allison
in 1972**

"Well, we got nine and you can't score more than that."

Sir Bobby Robson on a 9–0 thrashing of Luxembourg in 1960, in which he played

"After 15 years, I'm an overnight success."

José Mourinho

"Newcastle had not won in 29 games and two plus nine is 11. While they were scoring the winning goals, I was running round the outside of the ground 11 times to lift the hoodoo. I arrived late and had no ticket. But the moment I got out of the car and touched the Highbury stadium, Ray Parlour was sent off."

Uri Geller inspires a Newcastle United victory that ended a 30-game winless run in London, December 2001

DEFEAT

"Winning all the time is not necessarily good for the team."
John Toshack

"I'm not disappointed – just disappointed."
Kevin Keegan

"Not many people can say they scored at the Bernabéu so I was quite pleased, although I don't know how happy [goalkeeper] Bobby Mimms was."
Alan Harper on his own goal in a 1987 Everton friendly with Real Madrid

"A lot of hard work went into this defeat."
Malcolm Allison

"We're football people, not poets, but obviously I'm disappointed with the result."
Mick McCarthy definitely not a poet

"We must have had 99 per cent of the game. It was the other 3 per cent that cost us the match."
Ruud Gullit

"If I didn't have a will to win or it didn't hurt anymore when I got beaten, I would have retired years ago."
Manchester City manager Stuart Pearce responds to being asked if a 4–0 defeat at West Bromwich Albion hurt

"If they hadn't scored, we would've won."
Howard Wilkinson

"I'm looking for a goalkeeper with three legs."
Sir Bobby Robson after Shay Given is nutmegged twice by Marcus Bent of Ipswich Town

"We have all had more fun than this. Have you ever known a colder night?"
Martin Keown after the defeat by Shakhtar Donetsk in Moscow, November 2000

"We lost because we didn't win."
Brazil's Ronaldo

"England were beaten in the sense that they lost."
Dickie Davis

"I just felt that the whole night, the conditions and taking everything into consideration and everything being equal, and everything is equal, we should have got something from the game – but we didn't."
John Barnes with some classic football-speak

"Two questions – why were England so poor, and if they were poor, why?"
Commentator Ian Payne

"England had no direction but more formations than a ballroom-dancing team."
Terry Butcher, unimpressed by England's defeat in Northern Ireland in 2005

"Their keeper played very well and it was not the best pitch, but I am not making excuses."
Graham Rix

"We didn't have the run of the mill."
Glenn Hoddle

"We pressed the self-destruct button ourselves."
Brian Kidd

"We mustn't be despondent. We don't have to play them every week – although we do play them next week as it happens."
Sir Bobby Robson after a 2–0 league defeat to Arsenal who Newcastle United were to face a week later in the FA Cup

"We climbed three mountains and then proceeded to throw ourselves off them."
Billy McNeill, Celtic manager, after winning 5–4 in a topsy-turvy European Cup-Winners' Cup tie with Partizan Belgrade, but going out on away goals on an aggregate 6–6 score in 1989

"The circus came to town but the lions and tigers didn't turn up."
Newcastle United's Kevin Keegan after losing at Old Trafford in December 1995

"I've only got two words for how we played out there tonight – not good enough."
Sir Bobby Robson lays down the law at Newcastle United

GREAT
PLAYERS

"I don't think there's anyone bigger or smaller than Maradona."
Kevin Keegan

"I worked hard all my life for this. Those who say I don't deserve anything, that it all came easy, can kiss my ar*e."
Diego Maradona

"I had the vote of the people. Pelé won by the book."
Diego Maradona

"If he thinks he's the best player of the century that's his problem."
Pelé on Maradona

"Enthusiasm is everything. It must be taut and vibrating like a guitar string."
Pelé on football ... or Viagra

"That was Pelé's strength – holding people off with his arm."
Ron Atkinson

"I think that France, Germany, Spain, Holland
and England will join Brazil in the semi-finals."
Pelé

"He cannot kick with his left foot, he cannot
head a ball, he cannot tackle and he doesn't
score many goals. Apart from that he's
all right."
George Best on David Beckham

"He [Zinedine Zidane] has the body of a bear,
the mind of a fox and, er, terrific skills."
Brian Moore

"One year I played 15 months."
Franz Beckenbauer

"I am God."
Eric Cantona

"I might have said that, but on the whole I talk a lot of rubbish."
Eric Cantona clears things up

Reporter: "Is Klinsmann Spurs' biggest-ever signing?"
Ossie Ardiles: "No, I was."

"I'm moody and grumpy most of the time."
Roy Keane

"The Laudrup brothers can turn on a herring."
Ian Payne

"I remember almost hitting the clock at Highbury and was ready to tell the manager that I wanted to go back on the wing, but I knew he believed in me and that was enough."
Thierry Henry was not always confident in front of goal

"He's a fantastic player. When he isn't drunk."
Brian Laudrup on Paul Gascoigne

Interviewer: "Would you like to be thought of as being as good as Rangers legends such as Paul Gascoigne or Brian Laudrup?"
Ronald de Boer: "Yes, they are probably at my level."

"Happy Birthday – any chance of a rise?"
Message from Alan Shearer in a card marking Sir Bobby Robson's 70th birthday

"One of my great regrets is that I got the chance to speak to Bill Shankly only the once. After I signed for Liverpool, John Toshack took me to Shanks' house to meet him. He gave me two pieces of advice: don't over-eat and don't lose your accent."
Kenny Dalglish

"Wisey said I think too much. But I have to do all his thinking for him."
Gianfranco Zola on Chelsea team-mate Dennis Wise

"The thing about Michael is that he is fast, if defenders lose him for a moment they can't recover. Once Michael goes, they never catch him. On top of that is his finishing. He is so cold, even colder than a Swede."

England boss Sven-Göran Eriksson drooling over Michael Owen

"How dare Martin O'Neill ask Rivaldo to go for a trial in America! That is an insult to my client and to football. People will be crying tears of laughter when they hear Celtic wanted to take Rivaldo on trial."

Carlos Arime, Rivaldo's agent, in June 2004

"We didn't go swapping our jerseys in those days. We only had two sets of jerseys – one set would be getting cleaned and we would be wearing the other set."

Celtic's Bobby Carroll on being unable to exchange jerseys with Ferenc Puskas after Celtic's match with Real Madrid in September 1962

"If you put that wee thing out on the park, you'll be done for manslaughter."
Jimmy Quinn, Celtic centre-forward, to manager Willie Maley, on first seeing Patsy Gallacher, the 5-foot 6-inch, 7-stone, future Celtic great in 1911

"Maka's normally a one-in-ten man. Most players score nine out of ten but he misses nine out of ten."
Chelsea's Frank Lampard on team-mate Claude Makelele's penalty success rate

"I'm more afraid of my mum than Sven-Göran Eriksson or David Moyes."
Wayne Rooney, when still an Everton player

"It took a lot of bottle for Tony [Adams] to own up."
Arsenal's Ian Wright on his team-mate's admission of alcoholism

"I never predict anything, and I never will."
Paul Gascoigne

"I don't make predictions. I never have done and I never will do."
Ian Wright

"I couldn't settle in Italy – it was like living in a foreign country."
Ian Rush

"I'm five short [of the Arsenal goalscoring record] – not that I'm counting."
Ian Wright

"I've had 14 bookings this season – eight of which were my fault, but seven of which were disputable."
Paul Gascoigne

"I've never wanted to leave. I'm here for the rest of my life, and hopefully after that as well."
Alan Shearer plans to haunt St James' Park

Interviewer: "Would it be fair to describe you as a volatile player?"
David Beckham: "Well, I can play in the centre, on the right and occasionally on the left side."

"It's different – it's not the same."

Ryan Giggs

"One accusation you can't throw at me is that I've always done my best."

Alan Shearer

"My parents have been there for me, ever since I was about 7."

David Beckham

"I definitely want Brooklyn to be christened, but I don't know into what religion yet."
David Beckham

"I have a good record there. Played one, won one, and hopefully it will be the same after Saturday."
Steven Gerrard crosses his fingers

"This is the one-off occasion and you can't get any bigger occasion than that."
Bryan Robson

"Everything in our favour was against us."
Tottenham Hotspur great, Danny Blanchflower

"That was in the past – we're in the future now."
A time-travelling David Beckham

"I was really surprised when the FA knocked on my doorbell."
Michael Owen

"It's going to be difficult for me – I've never had to learn a language and now I do."
David Beckham on his move to Spain

"It's not just the manager who makes the decision, it's the player who makes the decision. They both decide fifty-fifty to make a decision."
Ruud van Nistelrooy

"Over the years a lot of great players have left United – I'm sure the same will happen to me one day."
Roy Keane

"Djimi Traore had to adapt to the English game and he did that by going out on loan to Lens last season."
Ian Rush on Djimi Traore

MANAGERS

"Intelligence doesn't make you a good footballer. Oxford and Cambridge would have the best sides if that were true. It's a football brain that matters and that doesn't usually go with an academic brain. I prefer players not to be too good or too clever at other things. It means they concentrate on football."
Bill Nicholson

"It was a surprise, but a very pleasant one. I had not planned to become a football club manager."
Arsenal physio Bertie Mee on being appointed Arsenal manager

"It's an incredible rise to stardom; at 17 you're more likely to get a call from Michael Jackson than Sven-Göran Eriksson."
Gordon Strachan on Wayne Rooney

"If that lad makes a First Division footballer, then I'm Mao Tse Tung."
Tommy Docherty on Dwight Yorke after his Aston Villa debut in 1990. Eight years later he was sold to Manchester United for £12.6 million

"That's great, tell him he's Pelé and get him back on."

Partick Thistle manager, John Lambie, when told a concussed striker did not know who he was

"The chairman of Brighton wouldn't recognize Gareth Barry if he was stood on Brighton beach in the team strip, with a seagull on his head and a ball in his hand."

Aston Villa manager John Gregory dismisses the claim that Brighton made Barry as a player

"I just wanted to give them some technical advice. I told them the game had started."
Ron Atkinson explaining why he moved from the stand to the dug-out during a game with Sheffield United in 1993

"What was my highlight of the tournament? Bumping into Frank Sinatra."
Ron Atkinson on the 1994 World Cup

"I played with Ron [Atkinson] in about a hundred reserve games. And according to Ron, he was Man of the Match in 99 of them."
Former Aston Villa player Dennis Jackson on his contemporary Ron Atkinson

"He invented the banana shot. Trouble was, he was trying to shoot straight."
Ron returns the compliment with regard to Jackson's shooting abilities

"When you finish playing football, young man, which is going to be very soon, I feel, you'll make a very good security guard."
David Pleat advises a 17-year-old Neil Ruddock

"There will have to be a bubonic plague for me to pick Di Canio."
Giovanni Trapattoni

"I'll never be able to achieve what Tommy Docherty did and take Aston Villa into the Third Division and Manchester United into the Second Division."
Ron Atkinson puts the boot in

"Robert Lee was able to do some running on his groin for the first time."
Glenn Hoddle

"His management style seems to be based on chaos theory."
Mark McGhee on Barry Fry

"The day I got married, Teddy Sheringham asked for a transfer. I spent my honeymoon in a hotel room with a fax machine trying to sign a replacement."
Gerry Francis

"Our central defenders, Doherty and Anthony Gardner, were fantastic and I told them that when they go to bed tonight they should think of each other."
David Pleat

"This is an unusual Scotland side because they have good players."
Javier Clemente on the under 21s

"I can't imagine him jumping for the ball. One of his false eyelashes might come out."
George Graham on Tomas Brolin, the multi-million misfit he inherited from Howard Wilkinson in 1998

"He said just two words to me in six months – you're fired!"
Tomas Brolin on George Graham

"You're not a real manager unless you've been sacked."
Malcolm Allison

"George Graham was telling Lee Chapman that if footballers looked after themselves there was no reason they could not play until 35. Then he looked over to me and said, 'Well, maybe not you, Quinny.'"
Niall Quinn on his old Arsenal boss

"You sold yourself easier than a bloody prostitute."
Manchester City manager Joe Mercer not impressed with Dave Bacuzzi being given the run-around by Cardiff's Ronnie Bird back in 1966

"You're not a good player. In fact, you're a bad player. But I could make you into a fair player."
Malcolm Allison introduces himself to Franny Lee in 1967

"He can't head it! He can't pass it! He's no good on his left foot!"
Malcolm Allison attempting to put other managers off as they watch a young Colin Bell play for Bury as Manchester City frantically tried to raise the necessary funds in 1966

"I've told the players we need to win – so that I can have the cash to buy some new ones."
Chris Turner motivates his team

"He took his curiosity to extremes: it was not unknown for Struth to carry out simple surgical procedures himself on terrified footballers laid out on the dressing-room table at Ibrox."
Journalist Alex Murphy remembers Rangers manager Bill Struth

"It was my first-ever game against Celtic and Tommy Burns kept giving me encouragement, saying that I was having a good match and to keep it going. I couldn't believe it!"
Rangers' Derek Ferguson on unusually sporting behaviour during a Glasgow derby

"Scottish football is full of hammer-throwers."
Graeme Souness

"There are two ways of getting the ball. One is from your own team-mates, and that's the only way."
Terry Venables

"I've been asked that question for the last six months. It is not fair to expect me to make such a fast decision on something that has been put upon me like that."
Terry Venables on whether he would remain England manager after Euro 96

"You get bunches of players like you do bananas, though that is a bad comparison."
Kevin Keegan

"By the look of him he must have headed a lot of balls."
Harry Redknapp on Iain Dowie

"Have I got anything bad to say about him? Well, he got cautioned by the referee at Burnley once."
West Ham manager John Lyall on Trevor Brooking

"He floats like a butterfly – and stings like one."
Brian Clough has no problem finding something bad to say about Brooking

"I've just been given a video recording of the game and I'm going to tape *Neighbours* over it."
Harry Redknapp is not happy with West Ham's goalless draw with Southampton in 1995

"I like the look of Mourinho. There's a bit of the young Clough about him. For a start he's good-looking…"
Brian Clough in November 2004

"People are comparing him [Mourinho] to Brian Clough, but Cloughy had the sexual attraction of a plate."
Journalist and author Hunter Davies

"They had a dozen corners, maybe 12, I'm guessing."
Craig Brown

"I'm a firm believer that if the other side scores first you have to score twice to win."
Long-serving manager and FA Technical Director, Howard Wilkinson

"A contract on a piece of paper, saying you want to leave, is like a piece of paper saying you want to leave."
John Hollins

"In terms of the Richter scale this was a Force 8 gale."
John Lyall confuses his scales

"Our first goal was pure textile."
Partick Thistle great, John Lambie

"There are two great teams in Liverpool:
Liverpool and Liverpool Reserves."
Bill Shankly

"If Everton were playing at the bottom of my
garden, I'd draw the curtains."
Bill Shankly

"Don't worry, Alan. You'll be playing near a
great side."
**Bill Shankly to Alan Ball after he joined
Everton**

"Give them these when they arrive – they'll
need them!"
**Bill Shankly hands a box of toilet rolls to the
Anfield doorman before Everton arrive for a
derby game**

"With him at centre-half, we could play Arthur
Askey in goal!"
Bill Shankly on giant defender Ron Yeats

"Take that poof bandage off, and what do you mean you've hurt your knee? It's Liverpool's knee!"
Bill Shankly to an injured Tommy Smith

"Tommy Smith would start a riot in a graveyard."
Bill Shankly

"It's the equivalent to being with the prettiest woman in the world and only sleeping with her once a month. I prefer to sleep with someone slightly less pretty every night!"
Gérard Houllier's way of saying he didn't want the England job

"Tore's got a groin strain and he's been playing with it."
Alex McLeish

"In football, you can never say anything is certain. The benchmark is 38–40 points. That has always been the case. That will never change."
Steve Bruce

"We're in a dogfight and the fight in the dog will get us out of trouble. We are solid behind each other, and through being solid we will get out of trouble and, if that fails, then we will be in trouble, but that's not the situation here. We'll all get in the same rowing boat, and we'll all pick up an oar and we'll row the boat."
Sir Bobby Robson in Churchillian mode at Newcastle United in 2003

"We're developing our youth policy."
Kenny Dalglish after Ian Rush joined fellow veteran John Barnes at Newcastle United

"We tried everything to get him. Maybe they offered Sharon Stone."
Tottenham Hotspur manager Ossie Ardiles on failing to get Philippe Albert, signed by Kevin Keegan for Newcastle United

"You never sell the fur of a bear before you shoot it. I have brought my cannon with me."
A cryptic Ruud Gullit on his bid to sign French winger Ibrahim Ba

"If you can't stand the heat in the dressing room, get out of the kitchen."
Terry Venables

"An inch or two either side of the post and it would have been a goal."
Dave 'Harry' Bassett

"In football, if you stand still you go backwards."
Peter Reid

"The lads ran their socks into the ground."
**Sir Alex Ferguson on footwear issues at
Manchester United**

"We threw our dice into the ring and turned
up trumps."
Bruce Rioch takes a gamble

"The spirit he has shown has been second
to none."
**Terry Venables on defender Terry Fenwick's
drink-driving charge**

"To be really happy, we must throw our hearts
over the bar and hope that our bodies
will follow."
Graham Taylor

"Give him his head and he'll take it with both
hands or feet."
Bobby Gould

"Cole should be scoring from those distances,
but I'm not going to single him out."
Sir Alex Ferguson

"We're going to start the game at nil–nil and go out and try to get some goals."
Bryan Robson keeps it simple

"I can't see us getting beat now – once we get our tails in front."
Jim Platt

"As we say in football, it'll go down to the last wire."
Colin Todd

"Their football was exceptionally good – and they played some good football."
Sir Bobby Robson

"And I honestly believe we can go all the way to Wembley – unless somebody knocks us out."
Dave Bassett

"It's understandable and I understand that."
Terry Venables

"Outside of quality we had other qualities."
Arsenal great, Bertie Mee

"To be talking about vital games at this stage of the season is ridiculous, really, but tomorrow's game is absolutely vital."

Brian Horton

"What I said to them at half-time would be unprintable on the radio."

Gerry Francis

"If we played like this every week we wouldn't be so inconsistent."

Bryan Robson puts his finger on it

"I promise results, not promises."

John Bond

"Without picking out anyone in particular, I thought Mark Wright was tremendous."

Graeme Souness

"Klinsmann has taken to English football like a duck out of water."

Gerry Francis on the German striker

"Even when you're dead, you must never allow yourself just to lie down and be buried."
Gordon Lee plans a comeback

"We ended up playing football, and that's not our style."
Alex MacDonald

"Hagi is a brilliant player, but we're not going to get psychedelic over him."
Andy Roxburgh rules out a summer of love approach against Romania

"It's thrown a spanner in the fire."
Bobby Gould

"Home advantage gives you an advantage."
Sir Bobby Robson

"…when Flitcroft played for the A team, he had 'footballer' written all over his forehead."
Colin Bell on what marked Garry Flitcroft out from the rest

"I can count on the fingers of one hand ten
games where we've caused our own downfall."
Joe Kinnear

"If it had gone in, it would have been a goal."
Joe Royle

"I am often interested in players but I never say
so, although I am looking for a striker and a
midfield player."
Colin Todd keeps his cards close to his chest

"We are not putting our cape over the tunnel:
we are putting our cape *in* the tunnel."
Howard Wilkinson

"The way forwards is backwards."
Dave Sexton

"I like to think it's a case of crossing the i's and
dotting the t's."
Dave Bassett

"When a player gets to 30, so does his body."
Glenn Hoddle

"When you score one goal more than the other team in a cup tie it is always enough."
Former Italy coach and father of Milan great, Paolo, Cesare Maldini

"What he's got is legs, which the other midfielders don't have."
Lennie Lawrence

"Hartson's got more previous than Jack the Ripper."
Harry Redknapp

"The important thing is he shook hands with us over the phone."
Alan Ball

"I have a number of alternatives and each one gives me something different."
Glenn Hoddle

"With hindsight, it's easy to look at it with hindsight."
Glenn Hoddle

"I just wonder what would have happened if the shirt had been on the other foot."
Mike Walker

"Some of our players have got no brains, so I've given them the day off tomorrow to rest them."
David Kemp

"The beauty of cup football is that Jack always has a chance of beating Goliath."
Terry Butcher rewrites the Bible

"Of the nine red cards this season we probably deserved half of them."
Arsène Wenger

"We didn't look like scoring, although we looked like we were going to get a goal."
Alan Buckley

"We're down to the bare knuckles."
The ever-combative George Graham

"Davor has a left leg and a nose in the box."
Arsène Wenger on his Croatian striker

"Today's top players only want to play in London or for Manchester United. That's what happened when I tried to sign Alan Shearer and he went to Blackburn."
Graeme Souness

"I don't read everything I read in the press."
Dave Jones

"I was a young lad when I was growing up."
David O'Leary

"We are now entering a new millennium and football's a completely different cup of tea."
Dave Bassett

"It would be foolish to believe that automatic promotion is automatic in any way whatsoever."
Dave Bassett

"I was inbred into the game by my father."
A disturbing one from David Pleat

"If it comes to penalties, one of these two great sides could go out on the whim of a ball."
Peter Shreeves

"In football, time and space are the same thing."
Graham Taylor shows his scientific side

"Very few of us have any idea whatsoever of what life is like living in a goldfish bowl – except, of course, for those of us who are goldfish."
Graham Taylor

"I've seen players sent off for worse than that."
Joe Royle

"We can't behave like crocodiles and cry over spilled milk and broken eggs."
Giovanni Trapattoni

"The margin is very marginal."
Sir Bobby Robson

"I'm not superstitious or anything like that, but I'll just hope we'll play our best and put it in the lap of the gods."
Terry Neill, not superstitious

"We are really quite lucky this year because Christmas falls on Christmas Day."
Bobby Gould with some festive cheer

"I can't see us getting beat now, once we get our tails in front."
Jim Platt

"Being given chances and not taking them. That's what life is all about."
Ron Greenwood

"I felt a lump in my mouth as the ball went in."
A classic from Terry Venables

"Tim Sherwood has come in, done very well
and given us another string to the bow in a
different type of way."
Glenn Hoddle

"If we start counting our chickens before they
hatch, they won't lay any eggs in the basket."
Sir Bobby Robson

"Playing another London side could be an
omen, but I don't believe in omens."
George Graham

"We played a 4-4-3 formation, which we have
played before and never failed to win with it."
**Mark McGhee's new system looks like
a winner**

"Referees don't come down here with a
particular-flavoured shirt on."
Steve Coppell

"We are a young side that will only get younger."
Paul Hart

"You can't say my team aren't winners. They've proved that by finishing fourth, third and second in the last three years."
Gérard Houllier

"We changed to a back four and went 4-4-3."
Glenn Hoddle adopts Mark McGhee's extra player formation

"Although we are playing Russian Roulette we are obviously playing Catch 22 at the moment and it's a difficult scenario to get my head round."
Paul Sturrock is not alone

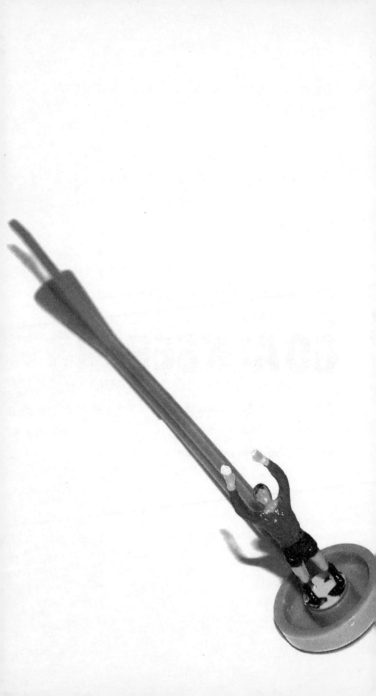

GOALKEEPERS

"To be marooned on a desert island with an
endless supply of lager, women and Sky TV."
Ian Walker describes his chief ambition

"It wasn't my choice to become a goalkeeper,
but I was probably too violent to play outfield."
Peter Schmeichel

"You shouldn't be nuts, but it doesn't matter
if you are a bit peculiar."
Peter Schmeichel

"The stars above Italian clubs' badges
show you how many times they have won
the Gazetta."
David James

"The lads used to call me 'the Judge' because
I sat on the bench so much."
Les Sealey

"That's a question mark everyone's asking."
Bruce Grobbelaar

"If you stand still there is only one way to go,
and that's backwards."
Peter Shilton

"What we have to do is put our teeth into the
Premiership."
Peter Schmeichel threatens the competition

"If you don't believe you can win, there is
no point in getting out of bed at the end of
the day."
Everton great, Neville Southall

"It's not nice going to the supermarket and the
woman at the till thinking, 'Dodgy keeper'."
David James on his loss of form in 1997

"I realize now that computer games have
affected my performance badly. The last time I
had a nightmare was at Middlesbrough in the
Coca-Cola Cup and I had played Nintendo for
eight hours beforehand."
David James

"Our goalkeeping coach, Joe Corrigan, has done a fantastic job on David's mental side. Though you'll never get that part completely right, because all keepers are mental anyway."
Roy Evans on David James

"I always dress from the left – left shinpad, left sock, left boot. It's stupid but I've always done it."
Paul Robinson

"If I had to choose between cricket and football it would be cricket every time."
Andy Goram, who was also Scotland's wicket-keeper

"I dreamt of playing for a club like Manchester United, and now here I am at Liverpool."
Sander Westerveld

"In football, you don't really know what is going on but we will worry about that when it happens."
Neil Sullivan

"Maybe the mistakes have looked worse
because they led to goals."
Ian Walker

"It was like déjà vu all over again."
Shaka Hislop

"If you make the right decision, it's normally
going to be the correct one."
FA Cup hero Dave Beasant

"Goalkeepers aren't born today until they're in
their late twenties or thirties."
Kevin Keegan offers an explanation

"Peter Schmeichel once asked for a shoe
horn. Schmikes keeps you on your toes every
match. It can take 20 minutes just to set out
his stuff. He doesn't always require the shoe
horn, but I keep it handy just in case."
**Norman Davies, retired Manchester
United kitman**

REFEREES

"It was like the ref had a brand new yellow card
and wanted to see if it worked."
Richard Rufus

"The referee was booking everyone. I thought
he was filling in his lottery numbers."
Ian Wright

"I never comment on referees and I'm not going
to break the habit of a lifetime for that prat."
Ron Atkinson

"I didn't know you were a Spurs fan."
**Blackburn Rovers boss Graeme Souness
to referee Graham Poll during the game at
Ewood Park with Tottenham Hotspur in 2003**

"I don't know about making referees professional.
They love themselves enough as it is now."
Paul Scholes

"This referee's so poor I'd have been booked
just getting off the coach."
Norman Hunter watching Mike Reed in 1998

"The referee in question was not one of my favourite people. In fact anyone who cr*ps in Graham Poll's toilet can't be all bad."
Referee Jeff Winter on the Robbie Savage toilet incident

"I can't take responsibility for the referee handing out bookings if people breathe too heavily."
Joe Royle

"The referee has a reputation for trying to make a name for himself."
Graeme Souness

"Don't talk about the game, talk about Uriah Rennie – that's what he likes and he's always been the same."
Kevin Keegan on his favourite referee

"I personally think referees should be wired up to a couple of electrodes and they should be allowed to make three mistakes before you run 50,000 volts through their genitals."
John Gregory

CHAIRMEN AND DIRECTORS

"A couple of people had told me that
[Birmingham City chairman] Ken Wheldon was
so tight that on rainy days he switched off his
windscreen wipers when he passed under
railway bridges."
Dave Mackay

"Chelsea has Roman Abramovich and his
millions made from Russian oilfields and
we've got Barry Hearn who does own a rather
lucrative snooker hall in Ilford!"
Comedian and Leyton Orient fan Bob Mills

"We have made an undertaking to Arsène
Wenger and his family not to name our
new coach."
Arsenal's Peter Hill-Wood

"Robert Maxwell's record is exemplary... He
has always been prepared to invest heavily in
football at a time when others are turning their
backs on the game. Some people seem to
doubt him, but they don't know the man."
**Tottenham Hotspur chairman Irving Scholar
in 1990**

"Our prices are half Newcastle's prices –
you just can't compare the clubs, they're
not to compare. We're stuck between a
massive city that's vibrant like Newcastle…
and Middlesbrough."
Sunderland chairman Bobby Murray

"The unthinkable is not something we are
thinking about at the moment."
**Then Manchester United chief executive
Peter Kenyon**

"You don't get this at Birmingham City."
**Aston Villa chairman 'deadly' Doug Ellis
introduces violinist Nigel Kennedy**

"It was a continuance of what we have seen
most of the season – that is, various clubs
beating each other."
Ron Noades on the essence of football

"Darren Anderton has had so many X-rays that
he got radiation sickness."
Alan Sugar

"I know more about schmaltz herring than I do about football."
Alan Sugar

"I'm a miserable sod."
Alan Sugar

"I've got a gut feeling in my stomach…"
Alan Sugar

"When I took over, football was not fashionable. Going into the bank and asking for money was like asking a rabbi to eat a bacon sandwich. Now the banks are queuing up to lend."
Alan Sugar

"I have found Alan Sugar to be one of the least charming people I have ever come across."
Arsenal chairman Peter Hill-Wood

"**Q:** What time is it?
A: Five past United!"
Chelsea chairman Ken Bates cracks a joke after Chelsea score five against Manchester United in 1997

"I had one agent phoning up saying, 'I have the honour of representing one of the world's greatest players, he needs no introduction.' I said, 'You're right, I don't want to meet him.'"
Ken Bates keeps his chequebook shut

"I am an accountant and I'm very suspicious of everyone in football."
West Ham chairman Terry Brown in 1998

"Women and horses work for nothing."
Doug Ellis on awarding himself a pay rise

"I don't want those scally City fans round at my house putting my windows in when City are in the Third Division and blaming it all on me."
Manchester City fan Noel Gallagher responds to suggestions he should become chairman

"Brian will hear anything on his position from me first."
Manchester City chairman Franny Lee shortly before he confirmed manager Brian Horton's sacking in 1995

"It's the first I've heard about it."
Brian Horton after reading he was out of a job in the morning paper

"We nearly didn't sign him because the letters did not fit on his shirt."
David Dein on the signing of Giovanni van Bronckhorst

"One of the directors said, 'If Davie's going to buy a couple of players the money will have to come out of his own pocket.' That epitomized their attitude at that time."
David Hay, speaking in 1995, on being manager of Celtic during the 1986–87 season

"He uttered the six worst words in the English language: 'I want to play for Liverpool.'"
Everton's Bill Kenwright on Nick Barmby after his switch of allegiance following Euro 2000

STADIUMS

"My mum always told me not to go near the main road."
Kevin Keegan during his first press conference at Manchester City

"Ashes? There will be six tons of lard left when they've done with me. Maybe they should pile me up by the posts. I might be able to help the goalkeeper."
Bernard Manning on the idea of having his ashes scattered at Maine Road

"We were supposed to come out at half-time to do a draw at Maine Road once but Frank Clark said, 'I don't want those two tossers on the pitch', and we respected him for that."
Radio 1's Mark and Lard explain how ex-manager Frank Clark endeared himself to them

"City have just built a fantastic multi-million pound new stand – the trouble is, it's facing the pitch."
Bernard Manning, 1995

"My first emotions on seeing St Andrew's
were not so much disappointment as disgust.
I remember walking out on to the pitch
and feeling I had stepped into a time warp.
You could wipe a finger down a wall and
inspect five generations of filthy dust.
It was hard to tell the broom cupboards
from the boardroom."

Karren Brady

"Ibrox really is a special place. It's incredible the bond fans have with parts of the ground. They can remember the day Baxter passed from here or there, and from where Gazza scored. I remember at training spotting little burnt areas. These were from people who had sneaked in at night and sprinkled the ashes of former fans on the pitch."
Rangers legend, Sandy Jardine

"I'll never play at Wembley again, unless I play at Wembley again."
Kevin Keegan says goodbye … or does he?

"I think a lot of people turned up because they wanted to see what people from Albania looked like."
Murdo MacLeod on the 51,000 crowd at Celtic Park for Glasgow Celtic's 1979 European Cup tie with Partizani Tirana, from the then secluded communist state of Albania

"When we came out for the match, the noise from the crowd nearly knocked us over."
Celtic's Willie Buchan on the European record crowd of 146,433 that saw Celtic beat Aberdeen 2–1 in the 1937 Scottish Cup final at Hampden park

"There were carloads of people arriving at the same time, all just to stand and stare in awe. I did myself, almost in a trance. I was reminded of the end of the film *Close Encounters of the Third Kind*, where people were simply drawn to the spaceship."
Comedian Bob Mortimer on the construction of Middlesbrough's Riverside Stadium in 1995

"During the afternoon it rained only in the stadium – our kitman saw it. There must be a microclimate here. The pitch was like a swimming pool."

José Mourinho, bewildered by the weather at Blackburn Rovers' Ewood Park, February 2005

"Going to matches at Highbury is like visiting church, it's the stuff of sustenance for the community's infrastructure. I love it on matchdays when the whole area becomes a sea of red. It's a special thing."

David Soul, aka Hutch, gets the Highbury bug

"You can't force people to sit down even if they have a seat. They want to sing and, unless you're Val Doonican, you can't do that sitting down."

Kevin Keegan on the crowd at Newcastle United's St James' Park

"With all those replica strips in the stands, coming to Newcastle is like playing in front of 40,000 baying zebras."
David Pleat, then Sheffield Wednesday manager

"For Newcastle United, the sooner they knock down this place the better."
Alan Shearer on the demolition of Wembley

FANS

"What a nightmare. I'm a Tottenham fan and I get cuffed to you."
A fellow prisoner to Tony Adams after the latter's arrest for drink-driving

"I vividly remember a nil–nil with Leeds. It was one of my all-time favourite matches – only an Arsenal supporter could say that of a goalless draw."
Ray Davies of The Kinks

"People said that I must have kept all the bricks that came through my window and put a snooker room on the side of my house. I did keep the bricks but I built a five-bedroom detached house in Wilmslow with them."
Steve Daley, 1979 British transfer record-holder, after life at Manchester City turned sour

"One of my most embarrassing confessions is that I'm a Chelsea fan – but the first time I ever went to Stamford Bridge was for a party thrown by Level 42."
Pop star Nik Kershaw

"When we had been there as players, two bad games and the fans were on your back; three bad games and they were rocking your car, trying to turn it over."
Alan Mullery remembers his days as a Tottenham Hotspur player

"You lose some, you draw some."
Comedian Jasper Carrott on being a Birmingham City fan

"We don't welcome yobs in any form, but that isn't to say we're against tribal loyalty. And our tribe aren't half fearsome when they want something."
Karren Brady on Birmingham City's fans

"The club call us hooligans, but who'd cheer them if we didn't come? You have to stand there and take it when Spurs are losing and others are jeering at you. It's not easy. We support them everywhere and get no thanks."
Tottenham Hotspur fan, quoted in *The Glory Game* by Hunter Davies

"Of all the roles Chelsea are expected to
fulfil – highest ticket prices in the league,
snazziest restaurant, chairman with the most
voluminous beard – winning the title is not
one of them."

**Jim White, writer and Manchester United fan
in October 1998**

"I remember a big fat red-haired bloke who
used to torture us at the start of every season
when it was boiling hot. He would lean over
the wall with his fat stomach showing and
a bottle of beer in his hand and leer at us
shouting, 'You're not fit!'"

**Francis Lee remembers a particular
Manchester City fan**

"Complaints, moans, complaints. Now listen to this bit: 'And you can tell Walter Smith to get his finger out of his ar*e.' And ar*e is spelt A-R-S-S."
Rangers chairman David Murray reads out a fan's letter to listening journalists

"Last Thursday we received a letter, dated next Monday, complaining about appalling language in the Shed at today's match against Everton. You have been warned!"
Chelsea chairman Ken Bates in September 1991

"I can't believe what I've seen tonight. It was a disgrace. If we'd have scored another goal in that atmosphere I don't think we would have got out alive."
Joe Royle after Manchester City's September 1998 visit to Millwall

"Even now when I'm asked for my autograph, I wonder if they were one of those who booed me."
Rangers' Ally McCoist remembers the bad times during his first stint with the club

"The worst crowd trouble I saw was down at Millwall. In the warm-up, there were people coming out of the crowd with meat-hooks in their heads. I think that's the only time I've been frightened in a game."
Chelsea's Ian Britton recalls a terrifying trip to The Den in 1976

"I've not renewed my season ticket, because I'm not going to give the directors my money. F*** them!"
West Ham fan and actor Ray Winstone

"Not so long ago, Boro were awful so I was always cracking jokes about them. But since they started doing well all my Boro gags have gone down the tube. Bryan Robson has a lot to answer for."
Comedian Roy 'Chubby' Brown

"It's good to be back at Wembley. We've been here 12 times. That's more than Chelsea."
Mick Jagger during The Rolling Stones 1996 world tour

"If I go home and find Massimo Maccarone in bed with my wife, I'm going to ask him if he wants another blanket."
Middlesbrough fan's reaction to the Italian's miraculous late winner that gave Middlesbrough a 4–3 aggregate UEFA Cup semi-final victory over Steaua Bucharest in April 2006

"When the ball's down the Kop end, they frighten the ball. Sometimes they suck it into the back of the net."
Bill Shankly

"You had to be strong to be on the Kop. When I was about 13, I tried to go in the middle where all the excitement was and almost got cut in half. I was only 5 foot 7 inches. A big docker pushed the crowd back and I ducked out and went back to my usual place to the left of the goal."
Elvis Costello

"I believe the last man to score five times in a Chelsea shirt was David Mellor."

Tony Banks MP, July 1997, after Chelsea had put five past Manchester United

"I picked up an injury and spent quite a lot of time on the bench. One of the supporters knitted me a cushion to sit on, which said, 'Reserved for Brian Kilcline'."

The man also known as "Killer" on home comforts at Newcastle United's St James' Park

"It was f****n' magic! When big Dunc Ferguson scored, I bloody exploded oot me seat, and so did Keegan!"

AC/DC singer Bryan Johnson recalls a visit to see his beloved Newcastle United

"I'm big on Aston Villa because the name is just so sweet. Other clubs are like 'Arrrrsenal' or 'Maaaan United' but Aston Villa sounds like a lovely spa."

Film star Tom Hanks

"What I don't understand is how a Frenchman can be playing for Manchester United. He's not even from England."
Lord Denning QC comments on the Eric Cantona bust-up at Selhurst Park

"Tony Banks described the English fans arrested in Marseille as brain-dead louts. This goes for me as well."
Labour MP Harriet Harman makes a slip

"I like watching matches, but I'm not certain about the scoring system."
Television presenter June Sarpong

"Do I support a London football team? I do. I support Manchester United."
Model and geographer Caprice

TERRACE SONGS AND CHANTS

"Tim Timminy, Tim Timminy, Tim Tim Teroo.
We've got Tim Howard and he says f**k you!"
**Everton fans celebrate their Tourettes-
suffering goalkeeper in the style of Dick
Van Dyke**

"We hate Tuesday."
**Millwall fans after Sheffield United fans chant
"We hate Wednesday" at Bramall Lane**

"Alvin, Alvin Martin, he's got no hair but we
don't care."
**West Ham fans chant for the popular defender
during the 1980s**

"Who let the frogs out, who? who? who? who?"
**Leicester City fans welcome Arsène Wenger's
Arsenal to the field**

"Two Andy Gorams, there's only two Andy
Gorams."
**Various opposition fans sympathize with
the Rangers goalkeeper after he had been
diagnosed with a mild form of schizophrenia**

"He's fat, he's round, he's sold your f**king ground, Al Fayed, Al Fayed…"
Various away fans at Fulham

"Bernt Haas. I've gone and Bernt my Haas. I've gone and Bernt my Haas. I've gone and Bernt my Haas. Bernt Haas…"
West Bromwich Albion fans enjoy their Austrian's player's name

"Whenever I'm in times of trouble, Mother Mary comes to me, Singing Glasgow Celtic 1, Caley 3. Celtic 1, Caley 3, Celtic 1, Caley 3, Glasgow Celtic 1, Caley 3."
Rangers fans rejoice in their old rivals' misfortune to the tune of "Let It Be"

"Rufus is a dog's name."
Queen's Park Rangers fans to their defender Rufus Brevett

"You're Shish, and you know you are."
Chelsea fans welcome Turkish side Galatasaray to Stamford Bridge

"It's just like watching Brazil."
Sung ironically by fans across the UK

"It's just like watching *The Bill*."
**Blackburn Rovers fans respond to a
particularly large police cordon**

"Joe Royle, Whatever you may do, You're
going down to Division Two. You won't win a
cup, You won't win a shield, Your next derby
is Macclesfield."
**Stockport County fans enjoy the relegation
of neighbour Manchester City to the tune of
'Lord of the Dance'**

"Niall Quinn's disco pants are the best,
They go up from his ar*e to his chest. They're
better than Adam and the Ants, Niall Quinn's
disco pants."
**Manchester City fans celebrate their striker's
fashion sense**

"You're just a small town in Burnley…"
**Manchester City fans taunt Blackburn Rovers
supporters at Ewood Park**

"Cannon and Ball are shagging your wife!"
Mancester City fans to Harry Kewell after his wife appears on "I'm A Celebrity…"

"Do the social know you're here?"
London clubs to visiting northern teams

"Oh, Teddy, Teddy. You went to Man United and you won f**k all."
Arsenal fans rib the former Tottenham Hotspur striker Teddy Sheringham after the Gunners win the Double in 1998

"I'm sure Arsenal fans are working on some new chants, but they can sing what they like. I've got three nice medals to show them."
Teddy Sheringham looks forward to his next match against Arsenal after winning the Treble in 1999

"Oh, Teddy, Teddy. You might have won the Treble but you're still a c**t!"
Arsenal fans prove Teddy right

"We all agree, Jaap Stam is harder than Arnie!"
Manchester United fans' chant at Sturm Graz's Arnold Schwarzenegger Stadium in December 2000

"There's only one Carlton Palmer and he smokes marijuana, He's 6 foot tall and his head's too small, Livin' in a Palmer wonderland!"
Stockport County fans serenade their manager

"When I first heard the fans chanting, I thought they were booing me. But I soon understood what they were saying and that they like me."
Kanu(uuuuuuu) on the early days at Arsenal

"Neville Neville, they're in defence, Neville Neville, their future's immense. Neville Neville, they ain't half bad, Neville Neville, it's the name of their dad."
Sung to the tune of David Bowie's "Rebel Rebel" at Old Trafford

"Don't blame it on the Biscan, Don't blame it on the Hamann, Don't blame it on the Finnan, Blame it on Traore. He just can't, He just can't, He just can't control his feet."
Liverpool fans blame it on the boogie

"Your sister is your mother, your uncle is your brother. You all fu*k one another, the Norwich family."
Visitors to Carrow Road

"We're supposed to be at home!"
Newcastle United fans singing in Barcelona in December 2002, after torrential rain saw their game postponed for 24 hours

"Come in a taxi, you must have come in a taxi.
Come in a taxi, you must have come in a taxi."
**Birmingham City fans salute a sparse
Sunderland away contingent**

"He's red, he's sound, he's banned from every
ground, Carra's dad, Carra's dad."
**Liverpool fans honour Jamie Carragher's dad,
once arrested for being drunk at a match**

"He's here, he's there, he wears no underwear,
Lee Bowyer, Lee Bowyer."
**Leeds United fans after Bowyer let slip that
he sometimes goes commando**

"Fat Eddie Murphy, you're just a fat Eddie
Murphy."
**Newcastle United fans take aim at Jimmy
Floyd Hasselbaink**

"He's here, he's there, we're not allowed to
swear, Frank Leboeuf, Frank Leboeuf."
**Chelsea fans censor themselves after
Leboeuf asked them not to swear when
singing about him**

"There's only one Emile Heskey, one Emile
Heskey. He used to be sh**e, but now he's all
right, Walking in a Heskey wonderland."
**Birmingham City fans enjoy their striker's
return to form**

FASHION
AND
HAIRCUTS

"I like the comfort of jeans and the elegance of a suit. But above all, I love the sensuality and sexuality that emanates from leather. It multiplies one's sensations tenfold."
Emmanuel Petit

"How can anyone say he's lazy? He is a sex symbol and has all that hair to blow-dry every day. That's an hour's job in itself."
Simon Mayo, Tottenham Hotspur fan and broadcaster, on David Ginola

"I think I'd like to be in the fashion industry. I don't really know anything about it, but I reckon I'm great at choosing clothes. The things I buy are the best clothes in the world – or at least that's what I think."
Paul Parker

"The lifestyle is much the same – bad clothing, bad food – so we don't expect too much."
Alfie Haaland on why Norwegians settle so well in England

"When I see all my legs out, I have confidence.
I look at my muscles and they look big and
I feel strong. With big shorts, I can't see my
muscles at all."
**Paulo Di Canio on why he wore unfashionably
short shorts**

"I swear that when we first walked out on
to the pitch most people thought we were
the band!"
**Robbie Fowler remembers the cream suits
worn by Liverpool on FA Cup final day in 1996**

"Barnesy's chucked me a couple of cast-offs, things he hasn't worn or he never really liked. A few years ago he gave me a jacket covered in the Chinese alphabet. I love it but it's a bit loud."
Barry Venison assessing Liverpool team-mate John Barnes' wardrobe

"José Mourinho sitting there smug and snug in his coat, the same one he's been wearing for twenty Januaries. Has he not heard of Oxfam?"
Hunter Davies, in the *New Statesman*, February 2005

"Is Chelsea's glory woven into José Mourinho's coat? Not since Joseph, the son of Jacob, has a coat acquired such symbolic significance."
Sarah Sands gets carried away in the *Daily Telegraph*, May 2005

"My hair is difficult, it's a problem! It doesn't always look healthy. But there's nothing I can do about it. If it was up to me I would have chosen a different kind of hair."
Every day's a bad hair day for Ricardo Carvalho

"I think I lost my barnet [hair] flicking the ball on for all them years at the near post from Brian Marwood's corners."
Arsenal's follicularly challenged Steve Bould

"In my time players had short hair, wore long shorts and played in hob-nail boots. Now they have long hair, short shorts and play in slippers."
Arsenal's "Gentleman" Jack Crayston recalls different times

"I think Pat's dress sense is dreadful. I would like to see him in a nice shirt or proper tie."
Mary Nevin, mother of former Chelsea winger Pat

"Luca wears some bad, bad underpants – like my grandfather wore. Big white underpants like they used 40 years ago."
Roberto Di Matteo on Gianluca Vialli

"Ed de Goey is the worst-dressed man I've ever seen. One pair of jeans, one pair of trainers, one shirt and one haircut."
John Terry on the Chelsea goalkeeper

"When I said I had no regrets I'd forgotten about that haircut and it has come back to haunt me on several occasions."
Former Everton and Rangers winger Trevor Steven on his permed mullet of the 1980s

"Never mix perms and drinking, it's a recipe for disaster."
Mick Lyons, former Everton captain

"My wife was a hairdresser and she decided to give me a new look. Nobody even recognized me when I went back and the commentators thought I was a new signing."
Everton's Paul Bracewell on his dramatic new barnet back in the 1980s

ANTICS

"No soup or pizza allowed inside for
safety reasons."
**Sign at away dressing room when Arsenal
visited Man City after the 'Battle of the Buffet'**

"At White Hart Lane, the two teams were going
down the tunnel and I felt this tugging from
behind. As I was about to step on to the pitch
with 30,000 people watching, Gazza was
trying to pull my shorts down. Luckily, they
were tied firmly or I would have made my
entrance with my kecks around my ankles."
David Seaman

"Gary Kelly is the maddest one at Leeds United.
Without prompting he was climbing headfirst
into wheelie bins."
**Paul Robinson remembers a Leeds United
Christmas outing in 1999**

"I was welcomed to Ibrox by McCoist
and Durrant spraying Ralgex all over
my underpants."
Iain Ferguson

"I do it at home, as well, strolling around like Tarzan in just a pair of Nikes. The neighbours know me pretty well."
Gary Kelly on team-mates' reports that he irons in the nude even when sharing a hotel room at away matches

"With Gazza around, you can expect to get pepper in your dessert and it has been known for him to book a sunbed for one of the black players in the squad."
Dennis Wise on England team-mate Paul Gascoigne

"I only went in for a filling and I came out drunk
– it must have been some anaesthetic! But get
the video tapes of that tournament and you'll
see how successful the dentist's chair was!"
**Paul Gascoigne, recalling an infamous
England squad drinking session prior to
Euro 96**

"The centre-forward's drunk, Mr Allison."
**Ted Drake to Arsenal manager George Allison
after he had just downed a bottle of lemonade
that was being used to highlight tactics**

"We had a lot of laughs. The one thing which really sticks out was the day that Micky Fenton got a brand new Jaguar. He was really proud of it and we thought 'We'll fix him.' So the groundsman, Wilf Atkinson, and I got a pail of whitewash and painted it all over Micky's new car. Micky wasn't too pleased!"

Middlesbrough's Rolando Ugolini recalls the antics of the 1950s

SOCIALIZING

"I don't really like the attention from girls – apart from anything else I already have a girlfriend. I like supporters of football whatever sex they are, but it's not so great when you're on a night out and girls just sit next to you … but to be honest it doesn't happen to me that often anyway."
Gary Neville

"Liz Hurley, she's nice. I'd take her to Pizza Express – no posh restaurants. We'd go for a pizza then to watch *Grease* or something."
Phil Neville describes his ideal date back in 1996

"I had more different women than I scored goals. And I scored 23 goals."
Aston Villa's Gary Shaw on his prolific 1980–81 Championship-winning season

Headwaiter: "Mr Allison, your bar bill – I have to tell you, it is enormous."
Malcolm Allison: "Is that all? You insult me. Don't come back until it's double that!"

"I always said that a team who drinks together, wins together."
Richard Gough

"We're actually quite a tame bunch. I don't think a Tuesday night out once every six weeks is excessive."
Robbie Mustoe debunks the myth of Middlesbrough as a drinking club under Bryan Robson

"The manager doesn't want me to live like a monk. If he tried to make me live like a monk my football would go down the drain. He understands that, we've had that conversation."

Dwight Yorke comes to an understanding with Sir Alex Ferguson

"I never socialized with Eric. My wife and I always said we would have him over, but we never got round to it. We always called round for the rent, but never to ask him over. That's terrible really, isn't it?"

Eric Cantona's former team-mate and landlord Mark Hughes

"Everyone thought Brian was clean-living. You should have seen him crawling along the hotel corridor, drunk, while on pre-season tour."

John Brown reveals how Brian Laudrup was welcomed to Rangers

"If he stays out of nightclubs for the next few years, he can buy one."
Gérard Houllier predicting a glorious future for Steven Gerrard

"I've only been to a pub once and that was to get cigarettes for my wife at 11.30 in the evening. I prefer bars to sit and drink tea or coffee."
José Mourinho gets into the swing of life in the UK, September 2005

"Although I like Japanese food a lot, until everything is cleared up I won't go back there."
Arsenal's Cesc Fàbregas, a regular diner at the London sushi restaurant where Russian spy Alexander Litvinenko is suspected to have been poisoned in late 2006

"There used to be a drinking culture in football and I know because I was part of it."
John Aldridge

"Andrew Flintoff. He's the man of the moment. He's just a normal, good lad and the best cricketer in the world. And I chose him because he got absolutely rat-ar*ed on the parade!"

Chelsea's Frank Lampard, nominating his favourite non-footballing sportsman, September 2005

"Modern-day newspapers would have had a field day just following Chelsea around. We wouldn't have been off the front or back pages."

David Webb on the 1970s side

"It was obvious from the moment we arrived in Baghdad and saw soldiers carrying machine guns that leisure activities would be limited."
Colin Pates on Chelsea's trip to Iraq, March 1986

"McEwans Best Scotch!"
John Hendrie, when asked what made him come to Newcastle in 1988

"Toon army, Malcolm Macdonald, Kevin Keegan, John Hall and Julie's Nightclub!"
Pundit Andy Gray names five things Newcastle

"If we invite any player up to the quayside to see the girls and then up to our magnificent stadium, we will be able to persuade any player to sign."
Sir Bobby Robson on the myriad attractions of Tyneside

"*Vaya ciudad* – what a town!"
Columbian striker Tino Asprilla after his first visit to Newcastle's famous Bigg Market

"We don't have reporters any more; we have QCs. Nowadays they aren't interested in how many goals a player scores, but where he's scoring at night."
Everton manager Joe Royle in 1994

"I hear Big Fergie likes a few pints, loves to stay out late and chase the birds and gives a bit of lip in training; in my book he has all the ingredients of a good footballer."
Jim Baxter, Rangers legend of the 1960s, on fellow Scot Duncan Ferguson

"Andy Gray is an ugly b*stard in the morning and I can vouch for that because I've slept with him a few times."
John Bailey recalls his Everton room-mate

"Every good team has a strong centre. I'd look round. Goalkeeper, Jim Cumbes. I'd think, 'What time did you get in last night?' Centre-half, Chris Nicholl. In the toilet putting his contact lenses in. Central midfield, Bruce Rioch. Shaking like a leaf. Centre-forward, Sammy Morgan. Next to Chris putting his contact lenses in. What chance did I have?"
Vic Crowe, Aston Villa manager of the early 1970s

"We were playing away and we'd taken this 15-year-old apprentice with us. As was the custom, a whisky bottle was passed round. Players took a drink, then when they'd gone on to the pitch Vic Crowe took a big swig. The apprentice asked him why and he replied, 'Son, when you're manager of this club you'll know why.'"
Jim Cumbes, Aston Villa goalkeeper in the early 1970s

WIVES AND GIRLFRIENDS

"It wasn't her wedding anniversary, it was her birthday, because there's no way I'd have got married in the football season. And it wasn't Rochdale. It was Rochdale Reserves."
Bill Shankly refuting stories that he had taken his wife Nessie to watch Rochdale on their wedding anniversary

"I do go to football sometimes but I don't know the offside rule or free kicks – or side kicks – or whatever they're called."
Victoria Beckham

"Who let the dogs out?"
Victoria Beckham as Dwight Yorke's then girlfriend Jordan takes her seat in the players' enclosure at Old Trafford

"God forbid if Alex Curran split up with Steve Gerrard. Who would she be then? You can't let a man make you."
Singer Jamelia, boyfriend of Millwall's Darren Byfield

"It's because I'm engaged to one of the most famous footballers in the country. I can't help that. She'll be glad to know I don't know her boyfriend's name but Steven thinks he's lower than a non-league football player."
Alex Curran hits back

"A master of the art of love-making."
Former FA secretary Faria Alam on Sven-Göran Eriksson

"We had a wonderful dinner. When we finished I was full of anticipation – but he wanted to clear the plates away first."
Faria Alam again

"I feel sorry for Nancy – not only does she look like a drag queen but she's latched on to someone who clearly doesn't love her."
Faria Alam on Sven's former partner Nancy Dell'Olio

"I can only believe what people say, he's frightened of her."
Sven conquest number two (that we know of) Ulrika Jonsson on Nancy Dell'Olio's hold over the unlikely lothario

"Well, it's only happened twice. That was it. But you see one betrays to launch a shout into the night."
Nancy Dell'Olio, in Cantona mode, on Sven's infidelities

"My parents really liked David and the kids, but they didn't like Posh. And when they met her family, they understood why."
David Beckham's former PA Rebecca Loos on Victoria Beckham

"I don't know much about football. I know what a goal is, which is surely the main thing about football."
Victoria Beckham

"I am not going to be no señorita."
Victoria Beckham on the prospect of moving to Spain

"I'm not materialistic. I believe in presents from the heart, like a drawing that a child does."
Victoria again

"I've already experienced worse moments in my life. It's a small problem, which needs time to be sorted out."
Ronaldo takes divorce in his stride

"He constantly wants sex because he thinks he can wear his groin out if it's being fixed. It's exhausting."

Harry Kewell's wife, Sheree Murphy, on what happens when your footballer husband has a pending groin operation

"I sorted out the team formation last night lying in bed with the wife. When your husband's as ugly as me, you'd only want to talk football in bed."
Harry Redknapp

"I don't have a thing for footballers."
Cristiano Ronaldo's on/off girlfriend Gemma Atkinson, formerly with Marcus Bent

HANDBAGS

"Greigy hit me once. I got up and then a moment later I was down again. Then seconds after that he dumped me on the track at Ibrox. I said to him, 'John, are you trying to intimidate me?'"
Celtic winger Jimmy "Jinky" Johnstone remembers Rangers' John Greig

"I didn't get that worked up in the dressing room. Instead, I used to read the programme to see who I had to kick that week."
Chelsea legend Ron "Chopper" Harris

"Nobby Stiles a dirty player? No, he's never hurt anyone. Mind you, he's frightened a few."
Sir Matt Busby

"I played against Ron Harris and he frightened the life out of me. Thankfully, he never whacked me, and I appreciate that."
Hull City manager Peter Taylor

"I like to think that, apart from being a bit of a butcher, I've something else to offer."
Ron Harris

"Tommy Docherty and Ron 'Chopper' Harris invented soccer violence. It's when they retired that it spread to the terraces."
Chelsea great, Peter Osgood

"Skilful as he was, Ossie could dish it out and I was no shrinking violet. We hated each other with venom."
Frank McLintock, captain of Arsenal's 1971 Double-winning team, on Peter Osgood

"I think John Terry's got a hell of a future. The only difference between him and me is that, when I tackled, they didn't get up."
Ron Harris

"I had more fights with Granty than anybody even though we were on the same team, even though we roomed together. He played for the jersey, even in training games."
Mick McCarthy on Peter Grant, his Celtic team-mate in the late 1980s

"Dennis Wise could start a fight in an empty room."
Sir Alex Ferguson

"He's grinning. 'You pr*ck.' He gestures dismissively. The red card comes out. Shearer's right. I am a pr*ck."
Roy Keane on an altercation with Alan Shearer

"Duncan Ferguson became a legend before he became a player."
Joe Royle

"I don't think the contact was as severe as the player made out. That part of the pitch was uneven, but it won't need any rolling now."
Everton manager Howard Kendall after Duncan Ferguson was sent off for "swinging an arm" at Derby County's Paulo Wanchope in 1998

"Everyone knows he is a crazy Celtic fan."
Rangers' Lorenzo Amoruso after a spat with Ayr United's James Grady

"Happy New Year, bhoys."
Rangers' Ally McCoist responds to Celtic
players unhappy with the way he went down
for a penalty in the first game of the year

"There was a lot of commitment in Celtic's
game, commitment, toughness and
aggression. I'm tempted to use another word
– but I won't."
José Mourinho after Porto's 2003 UEFA Cup
final victory

COMMENTATORS

"It's end-to-end stuff, but from side to side."
Trevor Brooking

"Julian Dicks is everywhere. It's like they've got 11 Dicks on the field."
Metro Radio

"For such a small man Maradona gets great elevation on his balls."
David Pleat

"Jean Tigana has spent the entire first half inside Liam Brady's shorts."
Jimmy Magee

"I think this could be our best victory over Germany since the war."
John Motson loses all perspective

"The lad got overexcited when he saw the whites of the goalpost's eyes."
Steve Coppell

"He's passing the ball like Idi Amin."
Alan Parry

"He's pulling him off! The Spanish manager is pulling his captain off."

Irish commentator George Hamilton

"Argentina are the second-best team in the world, and there's no higher praise than that."

Ron Atkinson

"Lee Sharpe has got dynamite in his shorts."

Stuart Hall

"Now Zola tries to inject some speed…"

Ron Jones

"That was only a yard away from being an inch-perfect pass."

Murdo MacLeod

"The World Cup is a truly international event."

John Motson

"That's an old Ipswich move – O'Callaghan crossing for Mariner to drive over the bar."

John Motson

"I would not say that he [David Ginola] is one
of the best left-wingers in the Premiership, but
there are none better."
Ron Atkinson

"He's not only a good player, but he's spiteful in
the nicest sense of the word."
Ron Atkinson

"They've picked their heads up off the
ground, and they now have a lot to carry
on their shoulders."
Ron Atkinson

"If history repeats itself, I should think we can expect the same thing again."
Terry Venables

"It's understandable that people are keeping one eye on the pot and another up the chimney."
Kevin Keegan

"I'd love to be a mole on the wall in the Liverpool dressing room at half-time."
Kevin Keegan

"We managed to wrong a few rights."
Kevin Keegan

"He transfixed the static Liverpool defence like a stoat on the rabbit."
Stuart Hall on Jimmy Floyd Hasselbaink in 1998

"That's often the best place to beat a goalkeeper, isn't it, between the legs?"
Clive Tyldesley

"When you speak to Barry Fry, it's like completing a 1,000-piece jigsaw."
Brian Moore

"They've flown in from all over the world, have the rest of the world team."
Brian Moore

"He must be lightning slow."
Ron Atkinson

"He'll take some pleasure from that, Brian Carey. He and Steve Bull have been having it off all afternoon."
Ron Atkinson

"There's lots of balls dropping off people."
Ron Atkinson

"The winners [of the Champions League] stand to make £10 million in prize money – that's before any money they can make on programme sales, hot dogs and the like."
Brian Moore

"Cantona's is speaking the whole French
dictionary without saying a word."
Barry Davies

"The Dutch look like a huge jar of marmalade."
Barry Davies

"And Rush, quick as a needle…"
Ron Jones on Liverpool legend Ian

"The Italians are hoping for an Italian victory."
David Coleman hits the nail on the head

"This is the first time Denmark has ever
reached the World Cup finals, so this is the
most significant moment in Danish history."
John Helm

"If Glenn Hoddle said one word to his team at
half-time, it was concentration and focus."
**Ron Atkinson commentating on England–
Argentina in 1998**

"It's headed away by John Clark, using his head."
Derek Rae

"Glenn Hoddle hasn't been the Hoddle we know. Neither has Bryan Robson."
Ron Greenwood

"If ever the Greeks needed a Trojan horse, it is now."
Gerald Sinstadt

"And now we have the formalities over, we'll have the national anthems."
Brian Moore

"The only thing Norwich didn't get was the goal they finally got."
A tongue-tied Jimmy Greaves

"He chanced his arm with his left foot."
Trevor Brooking

"Nicolas Anelka left Arsenal for £23 million and they built a training ground on him."
Kevin Keegan on what happens to Arsenal players who stray

"Welcome to Bologna on Capital Gold for England versus San Marino with Tennent's Pilsner, brewed with Czechoslovakian yeast for that extra Pilsner taste and England are one down."

Jonathan Pearce gets his priorities right

"Arsenal are quick to credit Bergkamp with laying on 75 per cent of their nine goals."

Tony Gubba does the maths

"Tottenham are trying tonight to become the first London team to win this cup. The last team to do so was the 1973 Spurs team."
Mike Ingham

"…so different from the scenes in 1872, at the cup final none of us can remember."
John Motson

"For those of you watching in black and white, Spurs are in the yellow strip."
John Motson

"And Seaman, just like a falling oak, manages to change direction."
John Motson

"It was the game that put the Everton ship back on the road."
Alan Green

"The Uruguayans are losing no time in making a meal around the referee."
Mike Ingham

"He's 31 this year: last year he was 30."
David Coleman

"One or two of their players aren't getting any younger."
Clive Tyldesley

"Madrid are like a rabbit dazed in the headlights of a car, except this rabbit has a suit of armour, in the shape of two precious away goals."
George Hamilton

"I'm sure coach Frank Rijkaard will want the Dutch to go on and score a fourth now – although obviously they'll have to score the third one first."
Angus 'Statto" Loughran

"There'll be no siestas in Madrid tonight."
Kevin Keegan

"I came to Nantes two years ago and it's much the same today, except that it's completely different."
Kevin Keegan

"In some ways, cramp is worse than having a broken leg."
Kevin Keegan

"He's showed him the left leg, then the right. Where's the ball, the defender asks? It's up his sleeve."
Clive Tyldesley

"Ziege hits it high for Heskey, who isn't playing."
Alan Green

"Ardiles strokes the ball like it was a part of his anatomy."
Jimmy Magee

"Well, Clive, it's all about the two Ms
– movement and positioning."
Ron Atkinson

"Xavier, who looks just like Zeus, not that I have any idea what Zeus looks like…"
Alan Green

"They [Bayern Munich] lost in the semi-finals
of the Champions League to Real Madrid last
year, and the year before that were beaten
in the final by Manchester United, so their
European pedigree is second to none."

Simon Brotherton

"David O'Leary's poker face betrays
the emotions."

Clive Tyldesley

"Their strength is their strength."

Ron Atkinson

"Jari Litmanen should be made compulsory."

Ron Atkinson

"The ball goes down the keeper's throat where
it hits him on the knees to say the least."

Ron Atkinson

"We haven't had a strategic free kick all night.
No one's knocked over attackers ad lib."

Ron Atkinson

"It slid away from his left boot, which was
poised with the trigger cocked."
Barry Davies

"A win tonight is the minimum City
must achieve."
Alan Parry

"He had an eternity to play that ball,
but he took too long over it."
Martin Tyler

"Ritchie has now scored 11 goals, exactly double the number he scored last season."
Alan Parry

"Wigan Athletic are certain to be promoted barring a mathematical tragedy."
Tony Gubba

"Welcome to the Nou Camp stadium in Barcelona, which is packed to capacity … with some patches of seats left empty."
George Hamilton

"John Arne Riise was deservedly blown up for that foul."
Alan Green

"It flew towards the roof of the net like a Wurlitzer."
George Hamilton

"The Everton fans are massed in the Station End, and Lee Carsley is attacking those fans now."
John Murray

"He is the man who has been brought on to replace Pavel Nedved. The irreplaceable Pavel Nedved."

Clive Tyldesley

"He's not George Best, but then again, no one is."

Clive Tyldesley

"The ageless Teddy Sheringham, 37 now…"

Tony Gubba

"Hagi has got a left foot like Brian Lara's bat."

Don Howe

"Hagi could open a tin of beans with his left foot."

Ray Clemence

"I'd say he's the best in Europe, if you put me on the fence."

Sir Bobby Robson

"The atmosphere here is literally electric."

John Motson

"And what a time to score! Twenty-two minutes gone."
John Motson

"Brazil – they're so good it's like they are running around the pitch playing with themselves."
John Motson

"Glenn is putting his head in the frying pan."
Ossie Ardiles

"England now have three fresh men, with three fresh legs."
Jimmy Hill

"Unfortunately, we don't get a second chance. We've already played them twice."
Trevor Brooking

"Stoichkov is pointing at the bench with his eyes."
David Pleat

"I think it's that lack of width with his height."
Trevor Brooking

"The Arsenal defence is skating close to
the wind."
Jack Charlton

"Brazil, the favourites – if they are the favourites,
which they are…"
Brian Clough

"They've missed so many chances they must
be wringing their heads in shame."
Ron Greenwood

"Merseyside derbies usually last 90 minutes
and I'm sure today's won't be any different."
Trevor Brooking

"Football's football: if that weren't the case it
wouldn't be the game that it is."
Garth Crooks

"And there's Ray Clemence looking as cool as
ever out in the cold."
Jimmy Hill

"He's got a brain under his hair."
David Pleat

"If there are any managers out there with a
bottomless pit, I'm sure that they would be
interested in these two Russians."
David Pleat

Jimmy Hill: "Don't sit on the fence Terry, what
chance do you think Germany has got of
getting through?"
Terry Venables: "I think it's fifty-fifty."

"He hit the post, and after the game people are going to say, well, he hit the post."
Jimmy Greaves

"He held his head in his hands as it flashed past the post."
Alan Brazil

"It's like a big Christmas pudding out there."
Don Howe

"Venison and Butcher are as brave as two peas in a pod."
John Sillett

"He was as game as a pebble."
David Webb

"Most of the players will be wearing rubbers tonight."
Gary Lineker

"They've come out with all cylinders flying."
Luther Blissett

"Germany are probably, arguably, undisputed champions of Europe."

Bryan Hamilton

"Fiorentina start the second half attacking their fans; just the way they like things."

Ray Wilkins

"In the words of the old song, it's a long time from May to December but, you know, it's an equally long time from December to May."

Jimmy Hill

"Like Jim Smith's [Derby] side this year, we were answering our own questions."

Kevin Hector

"Apart from their goals, Norway wouldn't have scored."

Terry Venables

"Manchester United have hit the ground running – albeit with a 3–0 defeat."

Bob Wilson

"That's no remedy for success."
Chris Waddle

"The World Cup is every four years, so it's going to be a perennial problem."
Gary Lineker

"He's not going to adhere himself to the fans."
Alan Mullery

"It's sometimes easier to defend a one-goal lead than a two-goal lead."
Mark Lawrenson

"Batistuta gets most of his goals with the ball."
Ian St John

"There won't be a dry house in the place."
Mark Lawrenson

"The candle is still very much in the melting pot."
Alan McInally

"All the cul-de-sacs are closed for Scotland."
Joe Jordan

"Hearts are now playing with a five-man back four."
Alan McInally

"The club has literally exploded."
Ian Wright

"He's like all great players – he's not a great player yet."
Trevor Francis

"Historically, the host nations do well in Euro 2000."
Trevor Brooking

"If Glenn Hoddle had been any other nationality, he would have had 70 or 80 caps for England."
John Barnes

"Kevin Keegan said if he had a blank sheet of paper, five names would be on it."
Alvin Martin

"He's a two-legged tripod, if you know what
I mean."
Graham Richards

"If Plan A fails, they could always revert to
Plan A."
Mark Lawrenson

"He was just about to pull the trigger on his
left foot."
Terry Butcher

"You either win or you lose. There's no
in between."
Terry Venables

"He's looking around at himself."
Jimmy Greaves

"Roy Keane, his face punches the air…"
Alan Brazil

"Those are the sort of doors that get opened if
you don't close them."
Terry Venables

"And for those of you watching without television sets, live commentary is on Radio 2."
David Coleman

"Chris Waddle is off the pitch at the moment – exactly the position he is at his most menacing."
Gerald Sinstadt

"If they play together, you've got two of them."
Dion Dublin

"Two–nil was a dangerous lead to have…"
Peter Beardsley

"The one thing England have got is spirit, resolve, grit and determination."
Alan Hansen

"He hasn't been the normal Paul Scholes today, and he's not the only one."
Alvin Martin

"He hits it into the corner of the net as straight as a nut."
David Pleat

"That was an inch-perfect pass to no one."
Ray Wilkins

"There's Thierry Henry, exploding like the
French train that he is."
David Pleat

"He's got two great feet. Left foot, right foot,
either side."
Alan Hansen

"I don't think anyone enjoyed it. Apart from the people who watched it."
Alan Hansen

"This is a real cat and carrot situation."
David Pleat

"He's got a great future ahead. He's missed so much of it."
Terry Venables

"Not only has he shown Junior Lewis the red card, but he's sent him off."
Chris Kamara

"These managers all know their onions and cut their cloth accordingly."
Mark Lawrenson

"Tempo, now there's a big word."
Barry Venison

"Let's close our eyes and see what happens."
Jimmy Greaves

"Craig Bellamy has literally been on fire."
Ally McCoist

"I think Charlie George was one of Arsenal's all
time great players. A lot of people might not
agree with that, but I personally do."
Jimmy Greaves

"That goal surprised most people, least of all
myself."
Garth Crooks

"Ian Rush unleashed his left foot and it hit
the back of the net."
Mike England

"He's perfectly fit, apart from his physical fitness."
Mike England

"That's bread and butter straight down the
goalkeeper's throat."
Andy Gray

"Roy Evans bleeds red blood."
Alan Mullery

"Every time they attacked we were memorized by them."
Charlie Nicholas

"It's a tense time for managers. They have to exhume confidence."
Gary Lineker

"He looks as though he's been playing for England all his international career."
Trevor Brooking

"You could visibly hear the strain in his voice."
Mike Parry

"The Belgians will play like their fellow Scandinavians, Denmark and Sweden."
Andy Townsend

"Michael Owen is not a diver. He knows when to dive, and when not to."
Steve Hodge

"The atmosphere here is thick and fast."
Chris Kamara

"The first two-syllable word I learned when I was growing up was 'discretion'."
Eamon Dunphy

"I watched the game, and I saw an awful lot of it."
Andy Gray

"Gary Neville was palpable for the second goal."
Mark Lawrenson

"PSV have got a lot of pace up front. They're capable of exposing themselves."
Barry Venison

"He's got a knock on his shin there, just above the knee."
Frank Stapleton

"There will be a game where somebody scores more than Brazil and that might be the game that they lose."
Sir Bobby Robson

"Solskjaer never misses the target. That time
he hit the post."
Peter Schmeichel

"At the end of the day, the team with the most
points are champions, apart from when it
goes to goal difference."
Tony Cottee

"Now they have got an extra yard of doubtness
in their minds."
Chris Kamara

"He's good at that, David Beckham. He's good
at kicking the ball."
Jimmy Armfield

"He is like an English equivalent of Teddy
Sheringham."
Trevor Brooking

"It's his outstanding pace that stands out."
Robbie Earle

"Their team is like a bad haircut, long up front but short at the back."
Robbie Earle

"The fact that Burnley got beat here already will stick in their claw."
Mark Lawrenson

"Wayne Rooney really has a man's body on a teenager's head."
George Graham

"He went down like a pack of cards."
Chris Kamara

"Peter Beardsley has got a few tricks up his book."
Ian Snodin

"He signals to the bench with his groin."
Mark Bright

"I saw him kick the bucket over there, which suggests he's not going to be able to continue."
Trevor Brooking

"They've forced them into a lot of unforced errors."
Steve Claridge

"You takes your money, you pays your choice, sort of thing."
Tim Flowers

"The one thing Gordon has brought to this team is a bit of work-rate and team spirit."
Robbie Earle

"If you had a linesman on each side of the
pitch in both halves you'd have nearly four."
Robbie Earle

"The goal that Charlton scored has
aroused Arsenal."
George Graham

"The managerial vacancy at the club remains
vacant."
Trevor Brooking

"Bridge has done nothing wrong, but his
movement's not great and his distribution's
been poor."
Alan Mullery

"I was in Moldova airport and I went into
the duty-free shop – and there wasn't a
duty-free shop."
Andy Gray

"And now for international soccer special:
Manchester United versus Southampton."
David Coleman

"More football later, but first let's see the goals
from the Scottish Cup final."
Des Lynam

"And now the goals from Carrow Road, where
the game finished nil–nil."
Elton Welsby

"If you were in the Brondby dressing room right
now, which of the Liverpool players would you
be looking at?"
Ray Stubbs

"He [Stan Mortensen] had a cup final named
after him: the Matthews Final."
Lawrie McMenemy

"The match will be shown on *Match of the Day*
this evening. If you don't want to know the
result, look away now as we show you Tony
Adams lifting the trophy for Arsenal."
Steve Rider

"This would cut hooliganism in half by 75 per cent."
Tommy Docherty

"We have more non-English players in our league than any other country in the world."
Gordon Taylor

"Football today would certainly not be the same if it had not existed."
Elton Welsby

"There's one that hasn't been cancelled because of the Arctic conditions – it's been cancelled because of a frozen pitch."
Bob Wilson

"It's end-to-end stuff, all at one end."
Jeff Stelling

"In the bottom nine positions of the league there are nine teams."
Ray Stubbs

"Arsenal could have got away with a nil–nil if it wasn't for the two goals."

Des Lynam

"Despite the rain, it's still raining here at Old Trafford."

Jimmy Hill

"There were two Second Division matches last night, both in the Second Division."

Dominic Allen

"Peter Shilton conceded five, and you don't get many of those to the dozen."

Des Lynam

"Chesterfield 1 Chester 1 – another score draw in the local derby."

Des Lynam

"It's a renaissance, or put more simply, some you win, some you lose."

Des Lynam

"Manchester United are looking to Frank Stapleton to pull some magic out of the fire."
Jimmy Hill

"In Scotland football hooliganism has been met by banning alcohol from grounds but in England this solution has been circumnavigated."
Wallace Mercer

"Kicked wide of the goal with such precision."
Des Lynam

"When I'm out on the pitch it's the closest thing to being back in a dressing room."
Steve Baines

"David [Johnson] has scored 62 goals in 148 games for Ipswich and those statistics tell me that he plays games and scores goals."
David Platt

"Our talking point this morning is George Best, his liver transplant and the booze culture in football. Don't forget, the best caller wins a crate of John Smith's."
Alan Brazil

INTERNATIONAL
DUTY

"International football is one clog further up the football ladder."
Glenn Hoddle

"Argentina won't be at Euro 2000 because they're from South America."
Kevin Keegan

"We probably got on better with the likes of Holland, Belgium, Norway and Sweden, some of whom are not even European."
Jack Charlton

"There's a slight doubt about only one player, and that's Tony Adams, who definitely won't be playing tomorrow."
Kevin Keegan

"Michael Owen – he's got the legs of a salmon."
Former Scotland manager Craig Brown

"After six weeks in the England camp, even Jack Charlton could look attractive."
**England 1966 World Cup winner
George Cohen**

"I was going to score an own goal, just to say I'd got a hat-trick at Wembley. Then Denis Law, who had played in the 9–3 game, told me that he would kill me if I did that."
Jim Baxter, who scored both of Scotland's goals in a 2–0 win over England in 1962

"If he had said anything to me after the game I would have punched him."
Andy Goram on Paul Gascoigne's goal in the 'Auld Enemy' game during Euro 96

"Everybody says Steve McManaman played on the left for me in Euro 96 but he never played on the left. The one time he did play on the left was against Switzerland."
Terry Venables

"I'm nervous about meeting so many new people. It's like when you go out with a woman for the first time – you're bound to wonder how it will end up."
Sven-Göran Eriksson before his first England game in 2001

"There is great harmonium in the dressing room."
Sir Alf Ramsey on his musical England side

"Germany are a very difficult team to play …
they had 11 internationals out there today."
Northern Ireland's Steve Lomas

"I want more from David Beckham. I want him
to improve on perfection."
Kevin Keegan

"We've got a monster around our neck after
beating England, but we must feed it."
Australia's Frank Farina

"Playing with wingers is more effective against
European sides like Brazil than English sides
like Wales."
Ron Greenwood

"A little bit the hand of God, a little the head
of Diego."
**Diego Maradona describing his first goal
against England at the 1986 World Cup**

"It wasn't the hand of God. It was the hand of a rascal. God had nothing to do with it."
England manager Sir Bobby Robson rejects the notion of divine intervention in Maradona's goal

"Malvinas 2 England 1! We blasted the English pirates with Maradona and a little hand. He who robs a thief has a thousand years of pardon."
Argentinian newspaper *Cronica* in 1986

"I knew my England career was not going to get off the mark again when manager Graham Taylor kept calling me Tony. That's my dad's name."
Mark Hateley

"Because of the booking I will miss the Holland game – if selected."
Paul Gascoigne

"The little lad jumped like a salmon and tackled like a ferret."
Sir Bobby Robson on Paul Parker's performances at the 1990 World Cup

"We didn't underestimate them. They were a lot better than we thought."
Sir Bobby Robson on England's 1990 World Cup opponents, Cameroon

"Eighteen months ago they [Sweden] were arguably one of the best three teams in Europe, and that would include Germany, Holland, Russia and anybody else if you like."
Sir Bobby Robson

"At the time it was really special, especially against the old enemy. In Scotland they try to erase the game from the memory; if you tried to talk about it they'd change the subject."
Jimmy Armfield on England's 9–3 victory over Scotland in 1961

"Everywhere I went people would shout at me, 'What time is it, Frank? Nine past Haffey.'"
Frank Haffey, Scotland's goalkeeper in the same game

"As we came round the corner from the 18th green, a crowd of members were at the clubhouse window, cheering and waiting to tell me that England had won the World Cup. It was the blackest day of my life."
Scotland striker Denis Law

"We owe the English big time. They stole our land, our oil, perpetrated the Highland Clearances and now they've even pinched Billy Connolly."
Gordon Strachan before the Euro 2000 play-off between England and Scotland

"I strongly feel that the only difference between the two teams were the goals that England scored."
Craig Brown

"We have faced African teams, we have faced English teams – so we are ready to face Scotland because we know what their play will be like."
Brazil's Mario Zagallo

"As I was heading towards goal, Alan Ball was shouting: 'Hursty, Hursty give me the ball!' I said to myself: 'Sod you Bally, I'm on a hat-trick.'"
Geoff Hurst recalling his memorable third goal in the 1966 World Cup final

"He looked like a pint of Guinness running around in the second half."
Paul Gascoigne's description of Paul Ince wearing a head bandage in a crucial match against Italy

"Shearer could be at 100 per cent fitness, but not peak fitness."
Graham Taylor

"What chance has any other top striker got with England while old golden boy Shearer is still on the scene? It's an issue which bugs me."
Andy Cole

"Swedes 2, Turnips 1"
Headline in *The Sun* after England lost to Sweden in 1992

"I used to quite like turnips. Now my wife refuses to serve them."
Graham Taylor

"England have the best fans in the world and Scotland's fans are second-to-none."
Kevin Keegan

"The 33- or 34-year-olds will be 36 or 37 by the time the next World Cup comes around, if they're not careful."
Kevin Keegan identifies a problem for international footballers

"If he was chocolate, he would eat himself."
Unidentified England player during Glenn Hoddle's reign

"I'm the man for the job. I can revive our World
Cup hopes. I couldn't do a worse job, could I?"
**Monster Raving Loony Party leader
Screaming Lord Sutch puts his name in the
frame for the England manager's job in 1994**

"Don Revie's decision doesn't surprise me in
the slightest. Now I only hope he can quickly
learn how to call out bingo numbers in Arabic."
**Football League secretary Alan Hardaker after
Revie, who was famous for organizing his
players' leisure time, left the England job to
manage in the UAE**

"I have to be honest and say that I felt Sir
Bobby Robson was a bit bumbling at times.
When I first turned up for training, he called
me Paul Adams."
Tony Adams in 1998

"'Wait until you come to Turkey' was the shout,
with fingers being passed across throats. And
that was just the kitman!"
**Gareth Southgate on Turkish reaction to an
England victory in 2003**

"The nice aspect of football captaincy is that the manager gets the blame if things go wrong."
Gary Lineker on being made England captain

"Michael Owen is a goalscorer – not a natural born one, not yet, that takes time."
Glenn Hoddle speaking at the 1998 World Cup

"I can't say England are sh*te because they beat us in the [Euro 2000] play-offs, and that would make us even sh*ttier."
Former Scotland striker Ally McCoist

"The Germans only have one player under 22, and he's 23."
Kevin Keegan on England's Euro 2000 opponents

"Portugal play football as I like to see it played. As a neutral it was fantastic. Unfortunately I'm not a neutral."
England manager Kevin Keegan after Portugal beat England at Euro 2000

"I feel I have broken the ice with the English people. In 60 days, I have gone from being Volvo Man to Svensational."
Sven-Göran Eriksson after his first game as England manager in 2001

"At last England have appointed a manager who speaks English better than the players."
Brian Clough reacts to Eriksson's appointment

"I have no doubts whatsoever that Germany will thrash England and qualify easily for the World Cup. What could possibly go wrong? The English haven't beaten us in Munich for a hundred years."
Former Germany player Uli Hoeness before England beat Germany 5–1 in 2001

"We went out with a whimper in the Brazil game. There was no fight. I'd rather you get Martin Keown on and put him up front and go out fighting."
Steve McManaman on England's 2002 World Cup exit

"We needed Winston Churchill and we got Iain Duncan Smith."

Anonymous England defender on Sven-Göran Eriksson's half-time team-talk during the England–Brazil game in 2002

"It was obvious England were overawed by Brazil, Brazil with ten players, men against boys. You could see England's body language at the end: 'We've done OK, haven't we? Got to the quarter-finals.'"

Roy Keane

"It's amazing what you can see through Sven's specs – I must get a pair."

Gary Lineker as Sven-Göran Eriksson attempts to gloss over another limp England performance

"We were encouraged to open ourselves to the Japanese cuisine on offer, but having been away from home for so long I could have died for a McDonald's."

Danny Mills on the England team's World Cup diet in 2002

"There have, of course, been worse moments
in English history – the Roman Conquest, the
Black Death, the Civil War, the fall of France
in 1940 and virtually the whole of the 1970s,
for example."

**Leader in *The Times* putting England's 2002
World Cup failure in perspective**

"With both penalties David Beckham snatched
at the ball like an adolescent golfer teeing
off in front of the clubhouse. The England
captain choked."

**Matthew Syed in *The Times* on Beckham's
Euro 2004 penalty misses**

"The good news is that Saddam Hussein is
facing the death penalty. The bad news is that
David Beckham's taking it."

Anonymous internet joke, 2004

TOP TEAMS

ARSENAL

"I didn't see that particular incident."
Arsene Wenger

"He's given us unbelievable belief."
Paul Merson on the magic of Arsène Wenger

"England boss Sven-Goran Eriksson was here,
so who did he watch then? Has he signed for
a different country?"
**Wenger wonders why Eriksson was watching
Arsenal field no English players against
Crystal Palace in 2005**

"Ray is without doubt the funniest player I've ever
trained with. It's so important to have players
such as Ray involved with the group, for his
contribution on the field and spirit off it. I only
wish I could understand more of what he says."
Gilles Grimandi on Ray Parlour

"To me, he will always be the Romford Pelé."
Marc Overmars on Ray Parlour

ASTON VILLA

"I'd like to play for an Italian club, like Barcelona…"
Mark Draper

"Someone asked me last week if I miss the Villa.
I said, 'No, I live in one.'"
**David Platt has no regrets after swapping
Aston Villa for Bari in 1991**

"He earned the name because of his
malodorous feet."
**Tranmere Rovers historian Gilbert Upton on
how Tranmere and Aston Villa legend Thomas
"Pongo" Waring came by his nickname**

"Aston Villa are seventh in the League – that's
almost as high as you can get without being
one of the top six."
Ian Payne

"He's fat, he's round, he's never spent a pound.
Doug Ellis, Doug Ellis"
Fans' chant

BLACKBURN ROVERS

"We're off to Wembley – you're off to Burnley."
Blackburn fans to West Ham

"I just kick a ball around."
Ryan Nelsen

"I've always said that I would love to manage one of the clubs I played for during my career."
Mark Hughes forgets his time as a player with Rovers.

"The game's gone soft. You see very few tackles being allowed."
Mark Hughes

BIRMINGHAM CITY

"Footballers are only interested in drinking, clothes and the size of their willies."
Karren Brady

"He doesn't know a goal line from a clothes line."
Barry Fry on David Sullivan

"If a jumbo jet was coming towards our area,
he'd try to head it clear."
Barry Fry Liam Daish

"If we are not careful we will be playing in
high heels and skirts and playing netball.
It is so frustrating."
Steve Bruce on referee Howard Webb

"It's about time us managers had a fight. I
wouldn't be daft enough to have a go at Sam
Allardyce but me and Bryan Robson would
be decent. I'd have to kill him or he'd keep
coming back at me!"
Steve Bruce

BOLTON WANDERERS

"Our major problem is that we don't know how
to play football."
Sam Allardyce

"If Ricardo Gardner should have been sent off, there should have been four players sent off for each side. So the match should have ended up six against six."
Sam Allardyce

"There was plenty of fellers who would kick your bollocks off."
Nat Lofthouse

CELTIC

"Celtic manager Davie Hay still has a fresh pair of legs up his sleeve."
John Greig

"There's as much chance of McAvennie leaving as there is of us losing 5–1 tomorrow."
Billy McNeill, Celtic manager, on 26 August 1988. Celtic lost 5–1 to Rangers at Ibrox the following day. Frank McAvennie was subsequently transferred to West Ham

"When I was at Celtic I was said to be a players' man and maybe that was true. In those days, if the ship was sinking I would have thrown all 11 lifebelts to the players. Now I would keep one for myself, throw ten and lose a player."

David Hay, former Celtic manager

"I don't believe everything Bill tells me about his players. If they were that good, they'd not only have won the European Cup but the Ryder Cup, the Boat Race and even the Grand National!"

Jock Stein on Bill Shankly

CHARLTON ATHLETIC

"I have always tried to look at the positive, even when you are in 10 miles of traffic on the M25."

Alan Pardew.

"Chim-chimeny, chim-chimeny, chim chim charoo. We hate the b*stards in Claret and Blue!"

Charlton fans enjoy a bit of local rivalry with this chant directed at West Ham United

"He was probably the best thing we did all day – apart from the penalty!"

Alan Pardew on the pre-match entertainment before Charlton beat Wigan Athletic in April 2007.

CHELSEA

That was not a football score, it was a hockey score…in training I often play matches of three against three and when the score reaches 5-4 I send the players back to the dressing room, because they are not defending properly."
Jose Mourinho on Arsenal 5, Spurs 4 in November 2004

"When he [Ashley Cole] joined Chelsea he had to sing for the other players. I printed out the lyrics of Sound Of The Underground. He didn't go for it but I know he really likes it."
Ashley Cole's other half Cheryl

"Yoghurts are down at Asda."
Chelsea's Graeme Le Saux, when asked for his 'Save of the Month' in September 1998

"For me, pressure is bird flu. I'm feeling a lot of pressure with the problem in Scotland. It's not fun and I'm more scared of it than football."
Jose Mourinho

"I said I wanted the same car as James Bond
and the reporter got the wrong end of the
stick and said I wanted to be James Bond!"
Joe Cole

EVERTON

"It was like guiding a rabid dog home."
**Journalist Ian Hargraves when asked by
Howard Kendall to keep an eye out for
Pat Van den Hauwe on a flight home from
pre-season**

"I think he's Uranian."
**Gordon Lee when questioned about Imre
Varadi's nationality**

"When I signed, I was told I was going to
be the first of many big money signings.
Someone was telling fibs".
**John Collins. 1999 after abandoning Monaco
for Merseyside**

"That's a home win and an away draw inside four days. We've only got one more game in November, and if we win that, I'm in grave danger of becoming Manager of the month."
Mike Walker. Four days before he was sacked in November 1994.

"I'm a hush puppy now."
Howard Kendall. After being called 'A young pup' by Brian Clough.

FULHAM

"Fulham Football Club seeks a Manager/Genius."
Newspaper article on Fulham's hunt for a manager in 1991.

"Let's say I play 4-4-2 at home against Portsmouth and we lose 0-3. Do I then start booing the fans?"
Chris Coleman sticks with 4-5-1 despite fans' chants

LEEDS UNITED

"A snarling angry Alsatian was literally inches away from my thigh before the police handler grabbed his head and pulled him away. As I ran on I shouted over my shoulder, 'I only crossed the ball – it's Lee Chapman you want, he's the one that put your team down.'"
Chris Kamara on the post-match pitch invasion after Leeds United won promotion at Bournemouth in 1990, simultaneously relegating their hosts

"I would not be bothered if we lost every game as long as we won the league."
Mark Viduka, then of Leeds United

"Once Tony Daley opens his legs, you're in trouble."
Howard Wilkinson

"Keep your hair short, your clothes smart and don't get caught up with loose girls."
Don Revie advising his squad on discipline

LIVERPOOL

"Aye, Everton."
**Bill Shankly to a barber who asked him if he
wanted anything off the top**

"If you're in the penalty area and don't know
what to do with the ball, put it in the net and
we'll discuss the options later."
Bob Paisley

"I daren't play in a five-a-side at Liverpool,
because if I collapsed, no one would give me
the kiss of life!"
Graeme Souness as his popularity waned

"I remember Jimmy Adamson crowing after
Burnley had beaten us that his players were
in a different league. At the end of the season
they were."
Bob Paisley

If a player is not interfering with play or seeking
to gain an advantage, then he should be."
Bill Shankly on the off-side rule

MANCHESTER CITY

"I rang my secretary and said, 'What time do
we kick off tonight?' and she said,
'Every ten minutes.'"
**Alan Ball during his troubled year as
Manchester City manager in 1996**

"He sees you when you can't even see yourself."
**Paulo Wanchope on (then) Manchester City
team-mate Ali Benarbia's passing abilities**

"I can't promise anything, but I promise
100 per cent."
Paul Power

"He arrived like a giraffe on roller skates."
**Rob McCaffrey's bizarre description of Niall
Quinn's equalizer in his debut for Manchester
City against Chelsea in 1990**

"It's true. I think he phoned our management office. There's no way he's ever getting them He scored against City on his debut."
Noel Gallagher explains why Ryan Giggs was denied complimentary tickets for a hometown Oasis concert

MANCHESTER UNITED

"Roy Keane is Damien, the devil incarnate off the film *The Omen*. He's evil. Even in training."
Ryan Giggs

"Juan is something special. Manchester United have bought a true great. There are few players in the world who you can say possess everything. But, yes, Juan Verón is one of those few. I believe he will one day be remembered as a true great of our game. United have got a player who can follow in the footsteps of all the legendary players they have had at the club."
Diego Maradona speaks too soon

"Nicky Butt's a real Manchester boy. A bit of a scallywag. He comes from Gorton where it is said they take the pavements in of a night-time."
Sir Alex Ferguson

"In 1969 I gave up women and alcohol. It was the worst 20 minutes of my life."
George Best

"We had a few problems with the wee fella, but I prefer to remember his genius."
Sir Matt Busby on George Best

NEWCASTLE UNITED

"I'm not going to look beyond the semi-final – but I would love to lead Newcastle out at the final."
Sir Bobby Robson

"I prefer it in Newcastle, knowing all the people want me here. They look me in the eye and say, 'I want to play with you.'"
David Ginola

"And they were lucky to get none."

Newcastle United legend Len Shackleton after the 13–0 defeat of Newport County in 1946

"I would have given my right arm to be a pianist"**Sir Bobby Robson**

"My father had five sons. I had four brothers"

Sir Bobby again

PORTSMOUTH

"Where are we in relation to Europe? Not far from Dover"

Harry Redknapp

"Have you ever seen a beach?"

Portsmouth fans to those of clubs not blessed with a seaside location.

"Get your nostrils,Get your nostrils, Get your nostrils off the pitch.."

Liverpool's Phil Thompson gets the Pompey treatment

Journalist: "Have you received any
death threats?'
Harry Redknapp: "Only from the wife when
I didn't do the washing up!

"Mansfield gave us one hell of a game.
I feared extra-time but we are still on
the march, still unbeaten, and I'm still
a brilliant manager!"
Harry Redknapp after a Carling Cup victory.

RANGERS

"You can't live in Glasgow and be called Nigel.
He's going to be Rab."
Ally McCoist on the arrival of Nigel Spackman

"The Italians are known for that, boss.
Fowl play."
**Ally McCoist after Graeme Souness warned
his players that the Italians once tried to
poison Trevor Francis' chicken dinner**

"Ladies and gentlemen of the jury… Oh, that was last week."

Ally McCoist at a supporters' do, a week after a brush with the law

"I have to say that I've never had any problems with Trevor's grip."

Rangers' Gary Stevens on rumours that team-mate Trevor Steven had a limp handshake

READING

"I can see where the referee was getting confused – he does look like so many of my players."

Steve Coppell on the sending off of club mascot Kingsley the lion – his Reading team kit was confusing the officials

"I'm not superstitious, but every time she comes we lose"

Steve Coppell wishes his mother would stay away from the Madejski Stadium

"I have always enjoyed watching English comedy programmes on TV – Mr Bean is the best. He is a crazy man. I bought the DVD as soon as I came to Reading and watch it every day after training."

Defender Andre Bikey

SHEFFIELD UNITED

Places like this [Bramall Lane] are the soul of English football. The crowd is magnificent, saying 'f*** off Mourinho' and so on."

Jose Mourinho

"It will be a cracking match and a close one – maybe decided by a referee's decision, an odd bounce or something like an over-the-line goal."

Neil Warnock

"I would buy some bad players, get the sack and then retire to Cornwall'

Neil Warnock on how he would manage Sheffield Wednesday

"Paddy didn't incite the Hull crowd. Anyway, we're going to report the 4500 people who called him a fat b*****d."
Neil Warnock defends Paddy Kenny against incitement charges

"Matches don't come any bigger than FA Cup quarter-finals."
Neil Warnock

SOUTHAMPTON

Reporter: "Welcome to Southampton Football Club. Do you think you are the right man to turn things around?"
Gordon Strachan: "No. I was asked if I thought I was the right man for the job and I said, 'No, I think they should have got George Graham because I'm useless.'"

"They are definitely among us and there is a massive conspiracy in place. I think there is a massive cover-up. There are also organisations in place far more powerful than governments.

And we don't know the truth because we can't handle it, the truth about alien existence would frighten people. They would rather ignore it than deal with it."
James Beattie whilst at the Saints

"I liken the current situation to that of the Starship Enterprise. The shields are up and the Klingons are shooting at us and every time they land a punch they are sapping our power."
Rupert Lowe continues the galactic theme

Reporter: "So, Gordon, in what areas do you think Middlesbrough were better than you today?"
Gordon Strachan: "What areas? Mainly that big green one out there…"

SUNDERLAND

"I started clapping myself, until I realized that I was Sunderland's manager."
Peter Reid after Dennis Bergkamp scores for Arsenal

"I still have enough belief in my managerial skills to believe I can turn things round."
Howard Wilkinson midway through Sunderland's record equalling nine consecutive defeats.

"Most importantly we are looking for someone we believe can improve our league position in the short term and secure our Premier League status."
Bob Murray sacks Peter Reid with Howard Wilkinson waiting in the wings

"We all know that we need someone in to help me up front. But whoever the manager brings in, I am sure he will be exceptional.
"Things have got to get better. If they don't get any better, we will be relegated."
Kevin Phillips fails to predict the arrival of Marcus Stewart and Tore Andre Flo

TOTTENHAM HOTSPUR

"I fell in love with this club and it still my favourite. I was made very welcome there by everyone and the fans were always marvellous. There is always a place in my heart for Tottingham Hotspurs."

Ossie Ardilles

"Wimbledon with fans."

Jimmy Greaves on Spurs under Gerry Francis

"We like a tackle at Tottenham. we're not pansies, you know."

David Pleat

"Man in the raincoat's blue and white army."

Spurs fans unable to utter the name of George Graham

"I was sitting just a few feet away from David Pleat at the World Cup. He's a nice fellow, but the man is mad: certifiably, eye-spinningly mad."

Radio presenter Danny Kelly

WATFORD

"We grow our players at this club, we don't have a greenhouse in the back because we can't afford it, we're more of a microwave club."

Aidy Boothroyd

"And sitting on the Watford bench is Ernie Whalley's brother Tom. Both Welshmen."

Brian Moore

"Elton John decided he wanted to rename Watford and call it Queen of the South."

Tommy Docherty

"It's the only way we can lose, irrespective of the result."

Graham Taylor

WEST HAM UNITED

"If you never concede a goal, you're going to win more games than you lose."
England and West Ham legend Bobby Moore

"Even when they had Moore, Hurst and Peters, West Ham's average finish was about 17th, which just shows how cr*p the other eight of us were."
Harry Redknapp

"With the foreign players it's more difficult. Most of them don't even bother with the golf, they don't want to go racing. They don't even drink"
'Arry again

"Dani is so good-looking I don't know whether to play him or f*ck him"
...and again

"Samassi Abou don't speak the English too good"
...and again

WIGAN ATHLETIC

"We won it 2 times, we won it 2 ti-iimes, Auto Windscreens we won it 2 times!"
Wigan fans trump Liverpool's "We won it 5 times" chants

It was like giants against Ken Dodd's Diddy Men.
Paul Jewell on facing the giants of Fulham

"Up front we played like world beaters – at the back it was more like panel beaters."
Paul Jewell on snatching defeat from the jaws of victory against Tottenham

"I have great respect for him and he has none for me."
Alan Pardew on Jewell